# HARVARD HISTORICAL MONOGRAPHS

## HARVARD UNIVERSITY PRESS

### CAMBRIDGE, MASS., U. S. A.

# HARVARD HISTORICAL MONOGRAPHS
## VII

PUBLISHED UNDER THE DIRECTION OF THE DEPARTMENT
OF HISTORY FROM THE INCOME OF

## THE ROBERT LOUIS STROOCK FUND

LONDON : HUMPHREY MILFORD

OXFORD UNIVERSITY PRESS

# BERNADOTTE

## AND THE

# FALL OF NAPOLEON

BY

FRANKLIN D. SCOTT

*Cambridge*

HARVARD UNIVERSITY PRESS

MCMXXXV

PRINTED IN THE UNITED STATES OF AMERICA

# CONTENTS

23481

# PREFATORY NOTE

THIS monograph is a condensation of a doctoral dissertation under the same title. Any who seek elaboration or verification on a particular point, or a more exhaustive bibliography, may refer to this unpublished work in the Harvard University Library. The question of Bernadotte's desire for the French throne is touched lightly here, because I have dealt with that in separate articles. The Norwegian aspects of Bernadotte's policy in 1814 have been curtailed on account of space.

Professor C. K. Webster interested me originally in this complex subject, and both he and Professor W. L. Langer have encouraged and aided me throughout. Two stipends from the American Scandinavian Foundation enabled me to carry on the research in European archives. Among the scholars and archivists who helped me I must mention particularly Dr. Herman Brulin of Stockholm, Dr. Emil Marquard of Copenhagen, and Rektor Sven Tunberg of Stockholm. I am grateful also for the special permission accorded me to use parts of the Bernadotte Family Archives.

Superior, Wisconsin
February 4, 1935

FRANKLIN D. SCOTT.

BERNADOTTE AND THE FALL OF NAPOLEON

# I

## BERNADOTTE, SWEDEN, AND EUROPE

### 1810-1812

SWEDEN, once imperial mistress of the Baltic, as late as 1800 possessor of over half the Baltic coasts, had by 1809 sunk to the nadir of her fortunes. She had been mutilated in territory by the Russian conquest of Finland, weakened economically by the turmoil of war and Napoleon's Continental System. She had been lacerated in pride by the ignominious defeats of war, and disrupted internally by the rule of the half-insane Gustav IV Adolf and the revolution which deposed him. Sweden seemed ready for the fate of Poland. But although she bent before the whirlwind she was toughened in purpose by a deep feeling of *revanche*. A careful and fortunate diplomacy could still preserve and resuscitate the state; an unsuccessful policy would extinguish it.

In this crisis of 1809-1810, Sweden obtained as Crown Prince and director of her foreign policy a French general, Bernadotte, distinguished *militaire* in his own right, marshal and Prince of Ponte Corvo by grace of Napoleon. An heir to the throne had to be elected quickly by the four estates of the Swedish realm because King Carl XIII, put on the throne by the 1809 revolution, was childless and senile. The government sent to Napoleon an appeal for advice, and hoped through him to obtain a leader who would, in alliance with France, eject Russia from Finland and reëstablish Swedish power in the Baltic. Strangely enough the master of Europe refused to meddle in the affairs of the north and the result was the election of Bernadotte. By a peculiar quirk of fate the Swedes mistakenly thought him Napoleon's choice, and rightly realized that he could help the troubled finances of the Swedish Riksbank. They elected for their future ruler a passive but intense rival of the French Emperor.

In an astonishingly brief time this new leader shifted Swedish policy away from its traditional friendship with France and its ingrained hostility to Russia into a system based upon war with France and alliance with Russia. Sweden, instead of recovering Finland and her Baltic supremacy, was to acquire Norway and an increased interest in western Europe.

Jean Baptiste Jules Bernadotte, Marshal of France, in 1810 renounced his titles and his religion and went north to found a new dynasty, the only "Napoleonic" dynasty which still survives. Born in 1763 in the district of Béarn in Gascony, Bernadotte was a "pure Gascon of Gascony"; "so complete an example of his race that he reproduced in his single personality twenty characteristic figures, Montluc and Cyrano, Henri IV and d'Artagnan"; "the most daring, the most extraordinary and the most fortunate of the cadets of Gascony." He was exceptional because in his case as in that of his hero Henry IV, there was grafted onto the bravado, charm and daring of the Gascon, the prudence and caution of the Béarnais.[1]

When Jean's father, an impecunious member of the *bourgeoisie honorable de la robe,* died in 1780, the boy ran off to the army. For ten years his rise from the ranks was steady but unspectacular. Then the Revolution broke, and opened to him new and unrestricted paths to glory. In battle he displayed the dashing courage of the Gascon, in politics the cool caution of the Béarnais and a firm loyalty to authority. Therefore the Terror watched him but passed him by. Soon he was a general and in 1797 it was he who led 20,000 reinforcing troops to General Bonaparte in Italy. There two spectacular leaders of men measured each other: Napoleon, ambitious, proud, cool, unscrupulous, avid for power; Bernadotte, ambitious too, but vain, emotional, loyal, avid only for glory. Soon Napoleon was to see in the Gascon general a possible rival in his own schemes. While Bonaparte went to Egypt Bernadotte was sent as ambassador to Vienna, where his bold flaunting of the revolutionary tri-color soon resulted in a riot and his expulsion from the Hapsburg capital.

Back in Paris Bernadotte quickly won in marriage the "pretty girl from Marseilles with the gay smile"— Desirée Clary, already the fiancée of Joseph Bonaparte, Napoleon, and Duphot. This marriage with Desirée was one of the most important events in Bernadotte's career, for as Napoleon said at Elba, there were probably at least three times when he would have shot

[1] The three quotations, from Albert Sorel, Comte de Vogüe, and Léonce Pingaud, are quoted by Sir Dunbar P. Barton, *Amazing Career of Bernadotte* (London, 1929), p. xiii.

Bernadotte had he not felt the bond of sentiment and clan through Desirée (for Julie Clary had married Joseph, and Bernadotte was thus within the outer circle of the Bonaparte family). The only child of the marriage was the son Oscar who was to succeed Bernadotte in 1844 as King of Sweden and Norway. Except for a few months in 1810-1811 Desirée herself remained in France until 1823; only faint traces can be discovered of her political activity during this period.

In the spring of 1799 Bernadotte had accepted office as Minister of War. He gathered war materials, re-animated troops and nation, and developed an organization largely responsible for the French victories of 1800 and 1801. Unfortunately for him he was not a politician. He was modest of his abilities and would not "try to force his destiny." He was also a devout respecter of constitutional authority. For these reasons Siéyès, plotting a *coup d'état*, had to get rid of him, and in September, 1799, the emotional and loyal Gascon was tricked into resigning his position of authority.

When General Bonaparte came back from Egypt he found that this man who would have tried to block him was out of office. He invited Bernadotte to join the group of the 18th Brumaire, but the strict constitutionalist stood aside. Frankly he told Napoleon that he disapproved of violent and unconstitutional methods, but he promised not to harangue the troops and not to take charge of an opposition movement unless called upon by the Directory; he would not usurp authority even to combat a usurper. Napoleon was satisfied, for it was the harangues he had feared.

In the next ten years Napoleon made every effort to "absorb" this man who was allied with his family by marriage and who was too prominent and too able to be pushed aside. Bernadotte was made a Marshal and Prince of Ponte Corvo; he was a division commander on Napoleon's campaigns into Prussia and Russia, at Austerlitz and Wagram. He was governor at different times in Hanover, Anspach and Hamburg, and showed himself an unusually efficient administrator and a surprisingly lenient master. As a contrast to the ordinary brigand type of officer he was long remembered, and in 1810 and 1813 the remembrance became a matter of significance. Moreover, throughout this period he maintained a frank independence toward Napoleon, and often visited the salons of Madame de Staël and Madame Recamier. He was loyal to the Emperor as Emperor, but he never disguised the fact that Napoleon was not his choice. He irritated Napoleon with tactless and exaggerated remarks, and Napoleon angered the sensitive Bernadotte by repeated attempts to throw on him undeserved blame.

In 1810 the Emperor was attempting to get this independent officer to retire to Ponte Corvo or to some distant command, when out of a clear sky dropped the offer of succession to the throne of Sweden. For Napoleon it was dangerous to have this man released from his ties to the Empire; for Bernadotte it was a relief to be freed from the shackles of obligation.

At the age of forty-seven Bernadotte went north to his new destiny. Some of his youthful dash had been subdued by experience; prudence had assumed a larger place in his character. He was a striking and dignified figure: tall and dark, with curly jet-black hair, piercing eyes and an aquiline nose. In the heat of sudden anger he had the impetuosity and arrogance of the Gascon soldier, ready with a torrent of words to submerge his antagonist. In his habitual reserve and calm he had the graciousness of manner of the Old Regime, with a charm that was irresistible. He was full of contrasts and extremes: boastful and modest, impulsive and calculating, confident yet infinitely suspicious. He was a born idealist, yet experience had taught him wariness. With all he was a painstaking, far-sighted administrator, and although not a brilliant tactician he was a superb leader of soldiers in the field.

As soon as Bernadotte, now named Crown Prince Carl Johan, arrived in Sweden (October, 1810) he began to take the controlling part in governmental affairs. This was facilitated by the old King's unexpected delight in the son who had been imposed upon him, and it was necessitated by the King's physical and mental incapacity.

Although matters of state centered in the Crown Prince there were of course ministers who advised. The minister for foreign affairs, Lars von Engeström, Chancellor of Lund University, was more scholar than politician. Well informed, able, he was lacking both in personal magnetism and in the breadth of view which makes a statesman. He was loyal to the Prince, and fell in with his policy, but disliked him personally. His feelings and opinions were hostile to Russia (partly because his wife had estates in Poland) and caused him to suspect a score of secret deceits in the Tsar's friendship for the Prince.[2]

The real backbone of Crown Prince Carl Johan's political system was the Chancellor, Erik af Wetterstedt. Wetterstedt was the ablest Swedish diplomat of the period, and almost the only man strong enough to make his personality felt alongside the overshadowing Prince. He had been private secretary to Gustav IV Adolf, but wisely remained passive at the time of the 1809 revolution, was soon accepted by the successful party, and at the age of thirty-two became chancellor. The office did not carry great authority, but Wetterstedt rapidly won an influence which Engeström never possessed. In 1809 he had already thought it might be best for Sweden to renounce hope of regaining Finland and expand to the west instead, through the aid of France. His influence may have had much to do with Bernadotte's policy toward Norway although Bernadotte's alliance system was the opposite of Wetterstedt's. Wetterstedt's work was behind the scenes, but his upright, clear-sighted, level-headed Swedish character sometimes provided for the state a bulwark against the impulsiveness of the Gascon.[3]

Neither Wetterstedt nor any other Swede could have carried through the policy now inaugurated, for jealousy and factionalism were rife among the nobles.

[2] Engeström reveals himself, unintentionally, in his *Minnen och Anteckningar* (2 vols., Stockholm, 1876).

[3] Prof. Hans Forssell wrote a first-class biography of the chancellor, *Minne af Statsministern Grefve Gustav af Wetterstedt* (Stockholm, 1889).

Although most Swedes hated Russia and admired France, the new Crown Prince had to assure the Löwenhielm brothers in December, 1810, that he would not allow Sweden to become a Napoleonic dependency. However, if he had at once come out against France he would have alienated the great mass of nobles and people. This might have aroused anew the turbulence which had resulted in the assassination of Gustav III, the deposition of Gustav IV Adolf and the recent murder of the dashing Fersén. Bernadotte had to work gradually, graciously, persistently, to convert men of divergent views to his program. He was admirably suited to the task: his foreign birth placed him outside the Swedish factions, and his personal magnetism won all parties of nobles and populace.

From his perch in Sweden in the autumn of 1810 Bernadotte looked down on a continent subjected to or in humble alliance with Napoleon; on Russia, whose ruin was being prepared; on Britain, fighting the long resultless struggle. For Sweden he felt neutrality to be impossible. Yet if Sweden sided with Napoleon he foresaw that she would be swallowed up by her ally or left to destruction by Russia. He saw as the alternative an alliance with Russia by which that country's advance would be limited to Finland, and Sweden permitted to compensate herself in the west. He considered Finland irretrievably lost. Sweden should accept this fact and instead win Norway and create a united peninsular state commercially dependent on Great Britain but politically independent. The conquest of Norway, thought Bernadotte, would gratify Swedish ambitions and give him the prestige necessary to consolidate his position.  The enlarged kingdom would be separated geographically from too-powerful Russia, it would have the "natural frontiers" dear to a son of the Revolution, and it would be divorced forever from continental turmoils.  Yet the conversion of the people to this program could come only through some offensive and shortsighted act of Napoleon himself; and the foolish deed was soon committed.[4]

The French occupation of Swedish Pomerania in January, 1812, suddenly alarmed Sweden into a realization of the danger from Napoleon.  This invasion was the culminating act in a long series of events. Basically the difficulty was that Napoleon was attempting to make Sweden enforce his Continental System, regardless of the fact that Sweden could hardly live if cut off from commerce with Great Britain.  For a time Sweden may even have profited by the destruction of trade in other states, for she became the great entrepôt for colonial goods smuggled to the continent. Then in the treaty ending her war with Russia in 1809 Sweden had been forced to accept the French commercial regulations, and in a treaty with France in January, 1810, she had to reiterate these pledges.  Nevertheless, despite these promises made for the sake of peace, she permitted scores of British ships to trade off Gothenburg and to smuggle British goods to the continent through Pomerania.[5]

[4] Swedish opinion was never thoroughly converted to the "Policy of 1812."  See Adolf Schück in the Swedish *Historisk Tidskrift* (1930), 231-232.

[5] See e.g., von Brinckman to Wellesley, Feb. 27, 1810, Baron von Schinkel, *Minnen ur Sveriges Nyare Historia* (ed. by K. V. Bergman, 12 vols., Stockholm, 1854-1855; and a *Bihang* ed. by S. J. Boëthius, 3 vols., Upsala, 1881-1883), *Bihang* II, 160; E. Heckscher, *The Continental System: An Economic Interpretation* (Oxford, 1922), 151, 160, 179, 264-265.

Napoleon's irritation deepened as the treaties continued to be flouted. He first agreed to allow Bernadotte six months time to reorganize Swedish administration before France took any new measures. He also asked Bernadotte to promise never to fight against France. Bernadotte protested against this condition as incompatible with his independent status, and it was withdrawn.[6] His protest evidently worried Napoleon, for on the very heels of the new Prince he sent an ultimatum to Stockholm: Sweden must not only enforce the Continental System, but declare war on Great Britain. The Emperor would allow the Prince no opportunity to prepare a re-orientation of Swedish policy. For Sweden in the autumn of 1810 there was no choice. War against France meant imminent destruction; war against friendly Great Britain could be declared but not fought, and even surreptitious commerce might continue. To placate France Sweden declared a war with her fingers crossed and fought it with her hands folded. Actual conditions remained as before.[7]

At this anomalous situation the blunt Alquier, French Minister to Sweden, became more and more incensed. He did not get on well with the Crown Prince, who complained that the minister talked like a Roman proconsul, and at last he had an open altercation with

[6] *Correspondance de Napoleon I<sup>er</sup>* (32 vols., Paris, 1858-1870), #16890; L. Lecestre, *Lettres Inédites de Napoleon I<sup>er</sup>* (2 vols., Paris, 1897 [2nd ed.]), II, 66. Tradition has it that when Napoleon yielded to Bernadotte's protest, he orated, "Go, and may our destinies be fulfilled." See also Czernicheff's despatch of October 21, 1810, *Sbornik imperatorskago russkago istoricheskago obshchestva* (Transactions of the Imperial Russian Historical Society), Vol. XXI (St. Petersburg, 1880), 1-21 (hereafter cited as *Sbornik*).

[7] O. Alin, *Carl Johan och Sveriges Yttre Politik 1810-1815* (Stockholm, 1899). Only Part I of this work was completed before the author's death.

foreign minister von Engeström.  With this event personal relations became impossible and Alquier was at
last removed to Copenhagen and M. de Cabre was left
in Stockholm as Chargé d'Affaires.  With both these
second-rate diplomatists Napoleon was definitely dissatisfied but unfortunately for him he found no others
to take their places.[8]  Nor did he exert himself to
conciliate his former marshal.  Bernadotte pointed
out that the welfare of Sweden depended on commerce,
and that her warehouses were overflowing with iron
while the people famished for lack of wheat.  For
months his appeals went unanswered, and the eventual
replies were evasive, flat.  For a year the Swedes continued to trade, and to favor British commerce, while
the French continued to protest.  Then suddenly
French troops invaded Swedish Pomerania, the continental entry for the illicit trade, and transported the
Swedish military detachment to France.[9]

This act of violence was the turning point in Swedish
policy—the turning point, perhaps, in Napoleon's fate.
The Swedes, despite their disregard of the Continental
System, had felt admiration and friendship for Napoleon.  If Napoleon's outrage in Pomerania had not
pulled the noose around Sweden's neck one jerk too
tight Bernadotte would have found it virtually impossible to align the Swedish people in a policy of
coöperation with detested Russia.  This invasion made

[8] Lagerbjelke (Swedish Minister in Paris) to King Carl XIII, March
19, 1810, Schinkel, *Minnen, Bihang*, II, 183-186; Napoleon to Bassano,
Nov. 22, 1811, Feb. 16, 1812, Paris AAE, N1790.  See also Coquelle,
"La Mission d'Alquier à Stockholm, 1810-1811," *Revue d'Histoire Diplomatique*, XXIII (1909), 196-239.

[9] Alin, *op. cit.*, chap. iv; Schinkel, *Minnen*, VI, 115n.

Swedish opposition to Napoleon imperative. The luxury of traditional hate had to give way before the necessity of self-preservation. Prince Carl Johan was ready for the change of opinion. Immediately his long-considered plans began to emerge into reality.

Nor was Sweden alone in feeling the oppressiveness of her French alliance. Prussia had been preparing secretly for years to break her fetters; Russia had found the Continental System disastrous and Alexander had been disillusioned in his "friend" Napoleon; Austria was "tacking, and twisting, and turning," only awaiting a perfectly safe moment to launch a fifth campaign against the French. Among the northern states Denmark alone was pro-French from her own choice. Yet in all the welter of discontent only Great Britain was actually at war with Napoleon, and she was at war also with Russia and Denmark and Sweden. A year and a half of bargaining, begging, and strife was to pass before the old bonds were completely snapped and the new alignment forged for the last coalition.

## II

### ALLIANCE BUILDING

#### *February 1812-April 1813*

No one, perhaps, saw more clearly the path ahead or
worked more persistently to break the trail than Carl
Johan, Crown Prince of Sweden. He was spurred on
by three fixed principles: his firm belief in the inevit-
ability of Napoleon's collapse; his conviction that
Sweden's economic well-being demanded the smashing
of the Continental System and close connections with
Great Britain; his personal necessity to do something
big for Sweden in order to establish himself and his
family securely in power. These ideas determined his
course of action from 1810 until 1814.

When Bernadotte first went north to the throne of
the Vasas the governments of Great Britain and Russia
looked askance; they feared he would be a puppet in
the hands of Napoleon. He did his best to reassure
them, but he was handicapped by the forced Swedish
declaration of war against Great Britain in November,
1810. However, as early as December, 1810, he assured Russia that he had no designs on Finland, and
his friendly statements perhaps influenced considerably
the defiant ukase of December 31, 1810, by which
Russia refused to be bound by Napoleon's commercial

decrees.[1]   With Great Britain Bernadotte's diplomacy
had little effect.  Mr. Edward Thornton was sent from
London in the fall of 1811 to negotiate with the Swedes,
but his instructions could not be reconciled with the
Swedish claims.  Bernadotte might never have made
more progress had not Napoleon, angered by the way
the Swedes flouted his Continental System, committed
the short-sighted outrage in Pomerania.  This one act
freed Bernadotte from any obligations to Napoleon
and from Swedish restraints, and also enabled him to
initiate negotiations with Russia and Great Britain,
for now he had a grievance.

Pomerania had been invaded January 27, 1812.  The
news reached Stockholm February 4.  Carl Löwenhielm, as friend and emissary of Bernadotte, braved
the Baltic winter and reached St. Petersburg February
18 to ask for a Russian alliance and thus to begin
the last coalition.  Negotiations proceeded with enthusiasm, for Russia needed to protect her rear and
marshal all her forces for her forthcoming contest with
the French.  A return mission to Sweden was des-
patched, but in St. Petersburg the eager Alexander
dealt directly with Löwenhielm and a treaty was signed
on April 5.  Sweden demanded a Russian guarantee
that Norway (then a kingdom joined with Denmark)
be annexed to Sweden; if threats to Denmark did not
gain it Russia was to furnish 15,000 men to help conquer it.  Only after she had obtained actual possession

---

[1] Czernicheff's reports of his conversation with Bernadotte in Stockholm
were sent to St. Petersburg just twelve days before this ukase was promul-
gated (*Sbornik*, XXI, 22-48).  See also *Mémoires du Lt.-Gén. de Suremain
1794-1815* (Paris, 1902); A. Vandal, *Napoleon et Alexandre I<sup>er</sup> L'Alliance
Russe sous le premier empire* (3 vols., Paris, 1891-1896), II, 510ff.

of Norway would Sweden send any troops to north Germany for a diversion against Napoleon—if it should then be necessary. To these bold demands Alexander agreed because he had to have Swedish friendship and perhaps also because he felt a certain remorse for his despoliation of Finland three years before.[2]

Napoleon had intended that his bold stroke in Pomerania should intimidate Sweden, and he had followed it with demands for 2,000 Swedish soldiers, the imposition of the French tariff with French overseers in Sweden, war against Russia, and reality in the phantom Swedish-British war. Bernadotte informed the Council of State of these conditions of vassalage, and said that if accepted "we must prepare, gentlemen, to sacrifice our political liberty"; the Council thereupon advised neutrality.[3] The ensuing declaration indicated clearly the reorientation of Sweden's policy.

Now Napoleon forgot his high-handed disregard of Sweden. Immediately he sent (March, 1812) proposals of alliance by Elof Signeul, Swedish consul in Paris, offering to Sweden the then Russian province of Finland, and promising to purchase a quantity of Swedish goods at Danzig. The offer was no inducement to Bernadotte: the prize was Finland, he wanted Norway; there was no subsidy; and the Crown Prince had high hopes of his negotiations with Russia and Great Britain.

[2] Alin, *Förhandlingar om allianstraktaten mellan Sverige och Ryssland av 5 April 1812* (Upsala, 1900); *British and Foreign State Papers, 1812-1814* (London, 1841), I, 306ff. See report from the Count St. Julien to Metternich, in N. Mikhailowitch, *L'Empereur Alexandre I^{er}* (2 vols., St. Petersburg, 1912), I, 500-504; also Engeström's *Rapport à Sa Majesté* of Jan., 1813.

[3] Carl Johan to Statsråd, Feb. 1812, SRA, C. J. Papper 88; from de Cabre, March 3, 1812, Paris AN, 1700; Statsrådsprotokoller (Resolutions of Council of State) for Feb. 21-24, 1812, SRA.

He replied by criticizing the past conduct of France, refuting the French arguments and offering mediation between France and Russia.[4]  It was not a humble response, yet it did not close the door, for Bernadotte was "broadminded" enough to wish to hear all sides— one could never tell what might happen.

The Emperor did send back a better offer, but still unofficial: Sweden would regain Finland and Swedish Pomerania, add some German territory including Mecklenburg and Stettin, and receive 6,000,000 francs plus 1,000,000 per month subsidy; Bernadotte personally would regain his French appanage of Ponte Corvo.[5]  Still Napoleon refused to tear Norway from his ally, Frederick of Denmark, and Bernadotte, fully aware of the fragility of Napoleon's power, sensed that he would soon be overthrown.  On the other hand, Great Britain still held aloof from Sweden, and Russia, ally though she was, wavered a little in May (1812). It was a time to be careful.

Back to Napoleon at Dresden went Signeul, with a response still oral—for the wisdom of experience made Bernadotte cautious to an extreme.  Signeul was to criticize the French proposals as vague and non-official,

[4] Schinkel, *Minnen*, VI, 141ff; Carl Johan to Napoleon, March 24, 1812, BFA; paper marked "Envoyées par Signeul le 28 Mars 1812," SRA, C. J. Papper 88.  A good summary is in F. W. Morén's *Kring 1812 Års Politik* (Stockholm, 1927), 19f.  See also B. Sarrans, *Histoire de Bernadotte . . .* (2 vols., Paris, 1845), I, 386-388, and M. Bail, *Correspondance de Bernadotte . . . avec Napoléon . . . 1812-1814* (Paris, 1819), 108ff.

[5] *Cambridge History of British Foreign Policy 1783-1919* (3 vols., Cambridge, 1922), I, 597; Morén, 36-38; Schinkel, *Minnen*, VI, 193ff; A. Ahnfelt, *Två Kronta Rivaler* (2 vols., Stockholm, 1887), II, 78-81; Scaevola, *Utländska Diplomaters Minnen . . .* (Stockholm, 1885-1886), 298-301; de Cabre to Bassano, May 15, Paris AN, 1700; *Meddelelser fra Krigsarkiverne* (9 vols., Copenhagen, 1893-1902), VI, 5.

and to ask why France should oppose the transfer of Norway, Sweden's "natural" acquisition. France should first of all restore Pomerania and respect the Swedish flag in the Baltic.[6] A reply to this new demand the exasperated Emperor never sent. In any case probably Bignon and Vandal are correct in their explanations of the move: that Bernadotte had no intention of leaving his allies, but wished to gain time and make sure of Norway in all contingencies. Perhaps above all he wished to force Great Britain's hand by a threat of Swedish alliance with the French.

Britain now became the state whose support was vital, yet both Russia and Sweden were technically at war with her. Worse than that, the British were still suspicious of the Gascon Prince, reluctant to grant huge subsidies to Sweden, and disgusted at the unblushing demands for Norway. Nevertheless in the spring of 1812 Mr. Edward Thornton was sent out anew.

Months of dickering eventually led to two simple treaties of peace dated July 18, 1812, at Örebro, Sweden—one between Sweden and Britain, the other between Russia and Britain. Sweden gained no alliance, for she held out for high terms: a guarantee of Swedish possession of Norway, the island of Zealand (on which Copenhagen is situated), and a West Indian

[6] From an untitled, undated paper in SRA, C. J. Papper 88. From "internal evidence" there can be no doubt as to the identification of the document. Schinkel quotes a different "Note Verbale" which he says exists in the Schinkel Samling. I could not find it. Bignon and Vandal quote still a different form as presented to Bassano: L. P. E. Bignon, *Histoire de France* . . . (10 vols., Paris, 1829-1838), X, 418-420; A. Vandal, *Napoleon et Alexandre*, III, 440-443; *Correspondance de Napoleon*, XXIV, 450; *Meddelelser*, V, 234. The *Journal de Malte*, for Aug. 26, 1812, has yet another version.

island; annual war subsidies of £1,200,000; all this prior to Sweden's action on the continent. As for Zealand, much as Bernadotte desired it he realized that British opposition would probably be insurmountable because of the fear of having a single power control both sides of the Sound.[7] Britain offered £1,000,000 provided that the dashing marshal would take a Swedish army to Germany at once, but if action was delayed only £500,000; to the Norwegian territorial guarantees she would not subscribe, and evidently did not even consider the question of Zealand. Deadlock resulted, for Bernadotte knew that in order to gain and hold Norway he must have at least the tacit consent of Britain and the support of the British fleet. While couriers wasted week after week between Stockholm and London the Russian auxiliary corps promised to Sweden lay idle, Napoleon marched on Moscow, and Bernadotte could do nothing but write Alexander stimulating letters advising that if necessary he retreat to the Caspian Sea.[8]

In order to hasten action the adventurous Admiral Bentinck at length helped to bring about a long-mooted conference between Alexander and Bernadotte.

[7] When Russia and Sweden planned their attack on Zealand they agreed that the future of the island would be discussed with Great Britain, and the Tsar waived his rights therein in favor of Bernadotte. (Treaty of Åbo, *British and Foreign State Papers*, I, 346ff., and see Schinkel, *Minnen*, VI, chap. vi. Treaties of Örebro in *British and Foreign State Papers*, I, 15ff.)

[8] *Correspondance inédite de l'empereur Alexandre et de Bernadotte pendant l'année 1812 publiée par X*, (Paris, 1909). Carl Johan promised to lead a Swedish army to the defense of Russia if the Tsar would give him temporary possession of Finland as a hostage for Norway (to G. Löwenhielm, Oct. 6, 1812, BFA). See also P. O. von Törne in *Historisk Tidskrift för Finland* (1925), 182-186.

Only these two eccentric geniuses could tell what magnificent dreams and practical schemes were broached when they met late in August, 1812, at the bleak Finnish castle of Åbo. We know only that promotion of Bernadotte to the throne of France was probably dangled before the eyes of an ambitious Crown Prince; that Alexander asked this same Prince to be his generalissimo, and was refused; that Bernadotte offered to participate immediately in the war if Russia would give over Finland as temporary security for Norway, and that this was refused; and that a marriage of Carl Johan's son Oscar with the seven-year-old Danish princess was suggested as a method of attaining peaceful Scandinavian unity. One practical gain was the signature of a treaty increasing the number of promised Russian auxiliaries to 35,000.[9] The most important result of the three-day meeting was the firm and lasting friendship there cemented between the two rulers of the north, between the visionary Autocrat of All the Russias and the revolutionary parvenu elected heir to the throne of Sweden, sworn enemy of Russia. This was an anomaly that was to make history.

Soon after Carl Johan returned to Stockholm he began a series of new appeals to Great Britain. He was gradually convincing Thornton of his sincerity. Now he wrote to the Prince Regent and sent Colonel Björnstierna on a special mission to London to plead for concessions before the campaigning season was past. He argued the absolute need of Norway in order to reconcile the Swedes to the loss of Finland, and thus

[9] The original terms had already been bettered by the Russians on June 15, Convention of Vilna, *British and Foreign State Papers*, I, 336ff.

to gain their coöperation in the new political system; he pointed out the advantage to Great Britain of forming a united Scandinavian state detached from the continent and dependent on British trade. As to method, if the Russian troops arrived the attack should be made on Zealand; if these forces were delayed Norway must be attacked directly; the British navy was essential in either case.[10]  Britain yielded reluctantly, and promised the help of the navy even against Norway, on the ground that Sweden deserved aid because she had restrained herself and allowed the Russian troops to be used in the common cause. Guadeloupe was offered to the hard-bargaining Prince, and Britain promised not to oppose the Russo-Swedish arrangements as soon as Sweden actually took part in the war against France.[11]

The British concessions came too late. When Björnstierna reached home all idea of autumn action had been abandoned and demobilization had begun. Napoleon had entered Moscow and Russia was prostrate. The Swedes feared that their government had made a ghastly mistake. The Crown Prince had to put up a bold front and wait for the fulfillment of his

[10] Carl Johan to the Prince Regent, Sept. 19, 1812, and to Björnstierna, Oct. 6, BFA. Björnstierna's note to Castlereagh, Oct. 6 (SRA, G. L. Sam.), shows how Bernadotte tried to win British approval for his conquest of Norway by pledges that it would be given autonomy and liberal institutions.

[11] Castlereagh to Thornton, Oct. 10, 20, 1812, London FO, Sweden 71; Björnstierna's notes, Upsala, Schinkel Sam., III; Morén, 47-50. And see *Supplementary Despatches, Correspondence, and Memoranda of . . . Duke of Wellington* (15 vols., London, 1858-1872), VII, 403-404. On the contributory mission of Gneisenau see M. Lehman, "Gneisenau's Sendung nach Schweden und England im Jahre 1812," *Historische Aufsatze und Reden,* 292-293; C. K. Webster, *The Foreign Policy of Castlereagh 1812-1815* (London, 1931), 105-106.

oft-asserted prophecy that the fall of Moscow marked the beginning of Napoleon's collapse. It was a desperate situation for Sweden as well as for Russia. A new Tilsit would have left both Prince and people at the mercy of the conqueror. But Alexander stood firm despite the intrigues of Romanzov, the hopes of the Danes, and the fears of the Swedes. Soon came the catastrophic retreat from Moscow, and the time was ripe for all northern Europe to rise against the lessening might of Napoleon. In the preliminary jostling for position the new Gascon Prince of Sweden had shown his independence, and the Swedish government had acted with an aggressive farsightedness which did much to restore her shattered prestige.

The creation of the new alliance structure proceeded so slowly through 1812 that Bernadotte was confronted with an additional problem: how to prevent Denmark from entering the alliance. If Denmark-Norway reversed her policy and joined the anti-Napoleonic coalition she could get a guarantee of territorial integrity from Great Britain at least and Carl Johan's plans to annex Norway would vanish like the mists of the morning. Bernadotte must see to it that until Denmark gave him Norway she remained in the opposing camp.

Denmark dared not and cared not to oppose Napoleon when he marched 600,000 men across northern Europe toward Moscow. But when the remnants of that horde staggered westward again the position of Denmark, on the flank of great military operations, became different. She was then of little value to

Napoleon because she had neither a good army nor able military leadership. But she was of potential value to the allies because of her proximity to the commercial and financial center of Hamburg. Incidentally, Denmark's importance seemed to increase as Sweden's decreased, for as the theater of war moved south and west Sweden was less and less of a possible threat to Russia.

Rosenkrantz, the able Norwegian-born foreign minister of Denmark, foresaw the probable course of events as early as September, 1812. Like Bernadotte he reasoned that the French occupation of Moscow was but a Pyrrhic victory. Foreseeing the expansion and ultimate success of the coalition he realized that if Denmark joined it early and fought valiantly the allies could not tear Norway away from her. He embodied these ideas in a memoir to King Frederick in September.[12] King Frederick, pinch-faced, proud, stubborn, was absolute ruler of his kingdoms, and he lacked the vision of his minister. Blinded by unreasoning hate of Great Britain, who had robbed him of his fleet and his colonies in 1807, he placed his full confidence in his ever-victorious and magnanimous friend Napoleon. He would not listen to Rosenkrantz' advice, but pursued the ruinous course of a wavering neutrality.[13]

Meanwhile, in St. Petersburg, the Francophil Rus-

---

[12] Memoir of Sept. 19, 1812, and Frederick to Rosenkrantz, Sept. 20, 1812, DRA. Summary in C. T. Sørensen, *Kampen om Norge i Aarene 1813-1814* (2 vols., Copenhagen and Christiania, 1871), I, 41f.

[13] Sympathetic but fair accounts of Danish policy are to be found in Sørensen, *op. cit.*, in Sørensen's later *Bernadotte i Norden* (3 vols., Copenhagen, 1904), and in E. Holm, *Danmark-Norges Udenrigske Historie, 1800-1814* (2 vols., Copenhagen, 1912).

sian Chancellor Romanzov was telling the Danish envoy, Otto Blome, that the Tsar had been seduced by the Gascon charmer but had no intention of fulfilling his pledge regarding Norway. At the end of November the Tsar himself told Blome that Denmark should abandon her alliance with France; if she did so and joined the coalition she could acquire Hamburg, Bremen, Lübeck, possibly even Holland, and become a power of the first rank; Norway would have to be given Sweden, he said, but only after Sweden's military action had earned her the right to it; would not Blome get instructions to treat with the Tsar personally and secretly?[14] Small wonder that the Dane thought Alexander wished to assure Norway to Denmark rather than to take it away. Even the cold and distrustful Lord Cathcart, British Ambassador to Russia, tried to become friendly and to suggest that if Denmark stood with Great Britain and Russia then Sweden would be powerless. Also the Spaniard Zea Bermudez tried to find a formula for the reconciliation of Denmark with the allies.[15]

But Bernadotte did not hibernate in his northern fastness. He realized keenly the danger to him of Danish accession to the alliance, and as soon as rumors reached him of the Russian negotiations he sabotaged

[14] Blome to Rosenkrantz, Aug. 27/Sept. 8 *et seq.*, 1812, DRA.

[15] Blome to Rosenkrantz, Nov. 24, 1812, DRA; Morén, 71-74. A little later Blome exulted over the discovery of a tactless letter written by Alquier, French Minister in Copenhagen, which he thought showed French contempt for Denmark; therefore Denmark could abandon the French alliance (Blome to Rosenkrantz, Nov. 27, Dec. 1, 1812, DRA). See *Meddelelser*, VI, 12-13; cf. Blome to Rosenkrantz, Nov. 13/25, Holm, "Nogle Akstykker . . . ," *Danske Magazin*, VI R. II B., 61-65.

them, for he was a bit suspicious of his Russian ally. The method he used was to state to Denmark immediately the conditions on which *Sweden* would admit Danish coöperation, conditions which of course included the preliminary transfer of Norway. A few days later (December 10, 1812) Oxenstierna, Sweden's Minister in Copenhagen, presented a formal note to the Danish government: if Denmark would cede Norway to Sweden and put 30,000-50,000 men in the field for the allies Sweden would coöperate to obtain for Denmark compensation in northern Germany; she would cede Pomerania to Denmark; she would renounce 2,000,000 riksdalers in commercial claims against Denmark and loan her another 2,000,000; and Sweden would like a family alliance.[16]

Consternation reigned in Copenhagen. The Russian play had been foiled four days before the Tsar's offer reached Denmark! Denmark could not now "sneak" into the alliance. Throughout the winter and the spring of 1813 Carl Johan kept bombarding Denmark with propositions, using as intermediary Baron von Suchtelen, Russian Minister in Stockholm, or Mr. Thornton, the British Minister, or dealing directly with Count Baudissin, the Danish chargé in Sweden, inviting Baudissin to dinner and exercising his potent charm to the limit. The impressionable young Baudissin did in fact come to think that expansion to the south was better for Denmark than retention of Norway, and thought that Denmark could reach a satisfactory agreement with Bernadotte by an appeal to

---

[16] Morén, 78, 81-82; *Meddelelser*, V, 273-275, VI, 16.

his heart, for the Prince was "open, straight-forward, and moved by those noble feelings which can best be expressed by the word knightly."[17] But both appeals and threats were unavailing, for, however different the phraseology of the Swedish demands might be, the demands themselves remained essentially the same. Sweden must have Norway, either at once or at the final peace.[18]

For months Denmark watched the net draw tighter around her and only waited, rejecting all Bernadotte's proposals, yet refusing also to be forced into an actively pro-French policy. She waited partly because of principle, partly because of royal stubbornness, and partly because she was out-maneuvered by Bernadotte. The first signs of a shift in policy appeared in January, 1813, when Rosenkrantz asked France for the relaxation of the Continental System: particularly withdrawal of French cruisers from Norway because they attracted too much attention from the British fleet, the release of Danish ships in the Baltic, and the lifting of postal restrictions at Hamburg; he hinted also at Denmark's desire for a general peace, and said Denmark could send no troops out of the country to aid Napoleon.[19]

[17] C. J. Anker, *Utdrag ur Danska Diplomaters meddelanden från Stockholm 1807-1808, 1810 och 1812-1813* (trans. by F. U. Wrangel, Stockholm, 1897), 196-200, (cited as Anker-Wrangel).

[18] Carl Johan complained that nothing could be done with Denmark because she was ruled by France through the hated Alquier. See *Correspondence, Despatches, and other Papers, of Viscount Castlereagh* (ed. by C. W. Vane, 12 vols., London, c. 1851), VIII, 332. Engeström to Löwenhielm, March 8, 1813, SRA, Musc., and to Rehausen, Apr. 1, 1813, SRA, Anglica. Alquier in turn complained he did not even know what was going on (to Bassano, Jan. 17, 1813, Paris AAE, D187).

[19] *Meddelelser*, VI, 7-11, 24-25. The French reply was conciliatory.

A few days later Rosenkrantz learned that Napoleon had accepted Metternich's proposals of mediation. Dared Denmark drift any longer? At the end of January the able heir-apparent, Christian Frederick, urged the King at least to make peace with Great Britain.[20] Rosenkrantz, too, once more sent in a pleading memoir, portraying the sad plight of Denmark wedged in between the Swedes, the British, and the advancing Russians. Adapting Romanzov's suggestion he advised that Danish troops replace the French at Hamburg and Lübeck before the Russians arrived.[21]

King Frederick at last yielded to the basic essential—peace proposals to Great Britain. But he demanded the complete restoration of his possessions and compensation for his losses of 1807; and in return all he would pledge was neutrality. Such terms were preposterous to a country not half as anxious for peace as Frederick thought she was; furthermore, the proposition did not reach England for a month—and that the very month when the British were finally coming to terms with Sweden. During that month Bernadotte was in a position to counteract the Danish move, for his Copenhagen spies had sent him immediately a summary of the note to London.[22] Castlereagh's reply was friendly, but merely referred the Danes to Thornton,

[20] Sørensen, Kampen om Norge, I, 61-63.
[21] Jan. 31, 1813, Meddelelser, VI, 17-20.
[22] Summary of Rosenkrantz' letter to Castlereagh is given by Engeström in despatches to Hegardt and to Löwenhielm on Feb. 12, 1813, SRA. Cf. Meddelelser, VI, 29-30. The Crown Prince's spies in Copenhagen did excellent service. Sørensen, Kampen om Norge, 66ff., and Morén, 131ff, give detailed accounts of the negotiations conducted by Sten Bille in London. Cf. also Alquier to Bassano, Feb. 9, 13, 20, 1813, Paris AAE, D187.

who had instructions; Britain was eager to do all possible consistent with her earlier obligation of which
Denmark was evidently informed.[23]

Negotiations on Swedish soil, even with Thornton,
were more than Frederick would stand. He decided to
try another special mission to London, this time by a
respected diplomat, Count Bernstorff, brother of his
Minister to Vienna. Still the King would not join the
alliance, and expressed fear of the judgment of history
on a man who deserted an ally at the critical moment.
In April Bernstorff bore to England a new set of impossible terms. Castlereagh said he had expected more
conciliatory proposals; he offered to conduct negotiations at Hamburg instead of in Sweden, but insisted
they must be carried on in concert with Russia and
Sweden; and then he said that the boat for Cuxhaven
would wait one day to take Bernstorff back. This practical expulsion of the Danish emissary was to calm the
apprehensions of Swedes, sorely troubled by the notori-
ous Dolgorouki mission in Copenhagen. Thus was allied
solidarity reaffirmed. Whatever advantage Denmark
had once held had been destroyed by her own procrastination, her excessive claims, and Bernadotte's
able manipulations.[24]

While with one hand Bernadotte repelled Denmark
from the coalition and held her in her French orbit,
with his other hand he beckoned to Great Britain.

[23] *Meddelelser*, VII, 39. This reply was known in Stockholm five days
before it reached Copenhagen.

[24] *Meddelelser*, VI, 64-65, 42-45; Rehausen to Engeström, to Carl Johan,
Mar. 2 *et seq.*, Engeström to Rehausen, Apr. 1, Cooke to Rehausen, Apr.
20, SRA, Anglica.

Sweden and Britain were uncommonly slow to reach an agreement because of mutual reserve and mutual suspicions. Sweden had recently experienced Russian perfidy at Tilsit, and Bernadotte had had wariness ingrained in him by twenty years of the French Revolution and Empire; Sweden hesitated to take any irretrievable step until she had definite British pledges. Britain, however, could hardly place confidence in a former French marshal until he was actually engaged in conflict with France, or at least had positively indicated his intentions, and she could not guarantee Norway to Sweden as Russia had done. Castlereagh proceeded to explain to Carl Johan the difficulties of parliamentary government:

"We [the British] can do much in support of foreign states (I believe no Power so much) but we must do it in our own way. The Continental Governments that have no account to render to a Parliament can commit themselves to engagements to guarantee possessions and never to lay down their arms until others are acquired well knowing that they are amenable to no authority for the prudence of such engagements and that when they become impracticable the engagements are dissolved either by circumstances or by mutual consent. They can also keep such engagements secret as long as it suits their convenience. In our system concealment is not practicable for any length of time, and when the stipulations are canvassed, they are impeached upon every extreme case that ingenuity can suggest . . . and the government charged with exposing the country to these inconveniences at the hazard of the nation's faith.

"It is not then to be inferred that the British government do not mean to maintain a point for a Friendly Power because they refuse to guarantee it. . . . This view of the subject ought at once to satisfy the Prince Royal and the

Swedish Gov't that if the support of Great Britain is the object aimed at, their endeavors ought to be directed not so much to press obnoxious stipulations, as by cordiality and common exertion to establish claims upon the gratitude of the British nation."[25]

Although such exhortations had small effect Bernadotte was at last forced to take the two preliminary steps Castlereagh demanded, for Sweden desperately needed Britain's support. This support had to be obtained before Denmark decided to shift position. Hence Carl Johan agreed to a treaty with the Spanish Bourbons, November 25, 1812, thus repudiating his brother-in-law Joseph; although this treaty, with the promise of a paltry subsidy and a contingent of 1500 men to Sweden, was never ratified, the gesture satisfied Britain.[26] Bernadotte's second step was to expel from Sweden the French chargé, de Cabre, (December 1812). Now Castlereagh was convinced that the Prince was playing square, and glad that Sweden had been "made to feel her diplomatic errors, without any diminution of friendly sentiments."[27]

Britain's satisfaction showed itself quickly both in the rejection of Denmark's advances and in the sending of General Alexander Hope to aid Thornton in negotiating an alliance with Sweden. General Hope

[25] Castlereagh to Thornton, Nov. 29, 1812, London FO, Sweden 71. For this quotation I am indebted to Professor C. K. Webster, who has printed part of it in his *Castlereagh*, 100-101; for an excellent survey of Anglo-Swedish relations in 1812 see pp. 92-102 of the same work.

[26] Great Britain would have paid the subsidy. Engeström to Rehausen, Jan. 4, *et seq.*, Rehausen to Engeström, Jan. 19, Feb. 16, 1813, SRA, Anglica. See Villa-Urrutia, *Relaciones entre España é Inglaterra* . . . (3 vols., Madrid, 1911-1914), III, 230-236.

[27] *Castlereagh Corr.*, VIII, 312-314.

arrived in Stockholm on February 11, 1813. The retreat from Moscow had reached its catastrophic climax, General Yorck's defection at Tauroggen (December 31, 1812) had signalled the upsurge of German nationalism, and the Anglo-Swedish negotiations were thus begun in an atmosphere of renewed hope and of confidence in Carl Johan's judgment.

The chief subjects in the ensuing discussions were Norway, subsidies, and campaign plans. All three of these items had long been agitated back and forth. On Norway Great Britain had decided to yield to Swedish insistence, to the extent, if necessary, of aiding its conquest with her fleet (but she did not guarantee possession). The subsidies question was troublesome, for the Swedes were both poverty-stricken and hard bargainers. They thought their army and their military genius-Prince were sufficient contributions, and that the financial sacrifice should come from wealthy Britain for the sake of a grateful Europe. After much haggling Sweden accepted the offer of £1,000,000 to keep her army of 30,000 until October, but she wanted £300,000 at once, and asked that £40,000 advanced for a separate expedition to Pomerania should be counted as an extra.[28]

Neither of the above agreements, according to Hope's instructions, was to take effect until the landing of the Swedish army "on the Continent." Hence the campaign plan became of prime importance. Bernadotte and the Swedes wanted a campaign which would gain early possession of Norway; the overthrow of Napoleon

[28] Engeström to Rehausen, Jan. 16 *et seq.*, 1813, Rehausen to Engeström, March 2, 9 (Ap. #2), SRA, Anglica; *British and Foreign State Papers*, I, 296ff.

was to them incidental if not distasteful. The British wanted a campaign which would quickly and effectively curb Napoleon's power; the Swedish acquisition of Norway was positively hateful to them. Yet each group could use the other for its purposes if the proper formula could be found, a compromise clause which would seem to give each nation its objective.[29] The compromise clause read:

"His Majesty, the King of Sweden engages to employ a Corps of not less than 30,000 men, in a direct operation upon the Continent, against the common enemies of the 2 High Contracting Parties. This Army shall act in concert with the Russian Troops placed under the command of His Royal Highness the Prince Royal of Sweden, according to stipulations to this effect already existing between the Courts of Stockholm and St. Petersburg."[30]

This sounds as if the British view prevailed, but what were the "stipulations to this effect" on which action was predicated? Basically, that Sweden should possess Norway before taking an army to Germany. By this undefined reference to his Russian treaties Carl Johan won approval for his plan of campaign. The vague clause quoted was for the benefit of the British public and the parliamentary system.

Privately between General Hope and Bernadotte a

[29] Instructions to Hope, Jan. 17, 1813, and Hope to Castlereagh, Feb. 14, London FO, Sweden 79. In an additional confidential instruction Hamilton, British Under-Secretary of State, specifically said that a Swedish approach to the continent via Copenhagen was a "waste of time and resources," and that if Carl Johan insisted on this movement the British alliance should be held in abeyance until the Swedes actually reached Germany (Jan. 19, 1813, London FO, Sweden 78). Evidently Hope did not mention to the Swedes the idea of an alliance held in abeyance.

[30] British and Foreign State Papers, I, 296ff.

detailed campaign plan was worked out, which provided for a British blockade of Zealand (with Copenhagen) and the landing of Swedish troops at both the
base and the tip of the Jutland peninsula—technically
"on the continent" but also in Denmark.  By this
plan Bernadotte could force Denmark to disgorge Norway and at the same time give valuable flank support
to the allied armies in Germany.  The plan had strong
strategic merits as well as political advantages, but it
was soon scuttled in the exigencies of the general
situation.[31]

Commercial interests were in the background in this
period of intense political strife, but they were not for-
gotten by either Sweden or Great Britain.  Bernadotte
had constantly in mind the close economic affiliation,
both present and future, of Sweden and Norway with
Great Britain, the chief market for northern timber and
ore and an important source of necessary supplies.
Partly economic was his and Sweden's desire for Guadeloupe, turned over by Great Britain to the Swedish

[31] "Projet donné confidentiellement à Monsieur le Général Hope,"
[March 4, 1813] signed "Charles Jean," London FO, Sweden 79; draft in
SRA, C. J. Papper 88, with appendices on transports, etc.  Hope, in a
despatch of Feb. 26 (FO, Sweden 79), upheld the idea of the aid to Russia
and Prussia from the flank position of the Swedish army, and enclosed notes
on Carl Johan's plans.  L. Tingsten in his *Huvuddragen av Sveriges Yttre
Politik . . . m.m., 1809-1813* (Stockholm, 1923), 50-51, is wrong on the
campaign plan, but F. W. Morén has written a good account in *Kunglig
Krigsvetenskapsakadamiens Tidskrift*, 1926, häfte 7-8, and a summary in
*Kring 1812 Års Politik*, 152-154.  Castlereagh's note to Carl Johan, Mar.
27, 1813 (SRA, C. J. Papper 88), unknown to Morén, implies that Hope
had made a binding oral agreement with the Prince.

There is no good evidence on the suggested diversion in Brittany, but
see Löwenhielm to Carl Johan, Jan. 17, 1813, and Suchtelen to Romanzov,
Feb. 13/25 (copy), (SRA, Musc.), and Hope's memorandum of Mar. 23
(London FO, Sweden 79).

royal family.[32]  Britain took care of her own interests
by obtaining entrepôts for her colonial goods at Gothenburg, Carlshamn and Stralsund.  Britain likewise insisted on keeping the Sound free from single-state control, for this might become a menace to British shipping
in the Baltic; therefore Sweden was not to be permitted
to get control of Zealand if Britain could prevent it.[33]

The treaty was received coolly in England, largely
because of the aid Britain promised for the transfer of
Norway.  Wellesley told Madame de Staël that the
"treaty has an air of injustice which will perhaps prevent its ever being executed."[34]  Castlereagh disliked
the whole proceeding, and waited until June to present
the treaty to Parliament, hoping Carl Johan would do
something spectacular in the meantime.  When he did
present it, however, he made one of the ablest speeches
of his career, and won approval by a large majority.[35]
The Swedish Council had ratified the treaty on April 2.
Disputes were to continue, yet each state had made a
useful agreement.  Britain had gained an ally against

[32] Britain could cede only her rights of conquest from France; a later
settlement returned the island to France and granted Bernadotte a money
compensation from Great Britain.  The Swedes also asked for any other
islands the British might have to give away (Thornton to Castlereagh,
Jan. 19, Feb. 14, 1813, London FO, Sweden 81; same to same, Mar. 4,
London FO, Sweden 78; Rehausen to Engeström, Mar. 30, Ap. #2, SRA,
Anglica).

[33] Article VI (*British and Foreign State Papers*, I, 296ff).  Colonial goods
were to pay 1% on entry, 1% on discharge; treaty to continue twenty years.
The government reminded Cathcart on Apr. 9 of the auspicious prospects
opening for British commerce (W. Oncken, *Oesterreich und Preussen im
Befreiungskriege* [2 vols., Berlin, 1876], II, 688).

[34] Mme. de Staël to Carl Johan, July (?), 1813 (copy), SRA, G. L. Sam.

[35] Rehausen's despatches, especially of Apr. 13, 1813, SRA, Anglica;
Castlereagh to Hope, June 6 (draft) London FO, Sweden 79; Webster,
*Castlereagh*, 145.

Napoleon, and Sweden could now place the British pledge alongside the Russian and consider that acquisition of Norway was assured.

Although Russia and Great Britain were Sweden's essential partners, the government recognized that coöperation with down-trodden but reviving Prussia was highly desirable. Prussia bordered on and coveted Swedish Pomerania, and lay near the line of communications for any Swedish army operating on the continent. Then, too, Sweden and Prussia were vitally interested in each other's future political and territorial adjustments, which in each case were significant for the eventual reorganization of all Germany.

To the very end of 1812 Prussia was in the chains of forced alliance with France and even in January, 1813, she broke off relations with Sweden at the behest of Napoleon. Yet Bernadotte kept in constant touch with Frederick William, and repeatedly urged him to respond to the rising insurgency of the Prussian nation. When Sweden's hopes were renewed by the negotiations with Great Britain Bernadotte promised to lead an army of 45,000 to act as the King of Prussia wished; but Prussia must decide soon, for her decision would force Austria and even Denmark to join the coalition.[36]

Irresolute Frederick William, forced on by the rising national sentiment, at length signed the treaty of

[36] Despatches of Tarrach (Prussian Minister in Stockholm), Berlin SA, I, 20; and his intercepted despatch of Jan. 8, in Paris AAE, S298; Goltz to Tarrach, Dec. 15, 29, 1812, Mar. 13, 1813, Berlin SA, I, 20; Engeström to Taube, Feb. 23, Apr. 5, 1813, SRA, U.S.K. A concise summary of events may be found in T. T. Höjer, "Sverige och det Tyska Rekonstruktionsproblemet vintern 1812-1813," *Historisk Tidskrift* (1933), 48-50.

Kalisch with Tsar Alexander (February 27, 1813). It took a few weeks more for him to muster up the courage to negotiate with Sweden and Great Britain. Then, to Bernadotte's surprise, Baron Jacobi-Kloest arrived in Stockholm, April 16, on his way to London. The old Prussian diplomat oiled the machinery of discussion by panegyrics on the grace, principles, and "divine fire" of the Crown Prince, and presented a letter from Frederick William declaring that

"it is to you, my Prince, that it is reserved to lead to victory a nation which has been already the liberator of Germany, and to recall by the glory of his arms the noble exploits of Gustavus Adolphus."[37]

The instructions Jacobi brought were not very liberal. Prussia had already assured Denmark of her opposition to Sweden's demand for Norway, hence this was not mentioned in the instructions; and Prussia assumed that Bernadotte was to come to Germany immediately. But under the changed conditions created by Swedish suspicions of the Dolgorouki Mission, and under the Gascon Prince's fascinating influence, the Prussian envoys were induced to sign a treaty far different from what their sovereign intended.[38] The treaty guaranteed Prussian aid in the acquisition of Norway, even with 15,000 Prussian troops if necessary. Prussian insistence on operations against Napoleon *"en premier lieu"* was dropped under Swedish protests. Not a word was said about the coveted Pomerania.

[37] SRA, Främmande Suveråners Bref til Carl Johan (cited as Främ. Suv.)

[38] The most detailed account of these negotiations is Einar Forssberg's *Sverige och Preussen 1810-1815* (Upsala, 1922), 65-75, although this dissertation is not entirely dependable.

In Germany Prussia would add 27,000 men to the Crown Prince's command. In return 30,000 Swedes would come to the continent and 25,000 would remain until Prussia was reconstituted as of 1806—geographically and financially. (Hanover, and the territory with which to compensate Denmark for the loss of Norway were specifically excepted from this article).[39]

This negotiation, dominated by the Swedes, and hurried by Jacobi's haste to reach London, came as a bitter disappointment to the Prussians. The failure to mention Pomerania, or to insist on immediate Swedish action against Napoleon was even worse than the detested acknowledgment of Sweden's claim to Norway. Therefore Prussian ratification was delayed for three months and Prusso-Swedish coöperation embittered from the very start.

Austria did not yield so easily. She played a coy rôle in the drama of diplomatic preparations. Chastised too often, she would be sure this time before she ventured battle. Despite fervent wooing by both military groups she kept herself unpledged until the summer of 1813, and with Sweden she signed no treaty until the war was over and Norway already won.

Austro-Swedish relations had not been pleasant since the spring of 1812, when Bernadotte had informed the Russians of the Austro-French alliance, and in resentment the Austrian Minister to Sweden, Count Neipperg, was withdrawn "on leave." He started back in

[39] B. von Quistorp, *Geschichte der Nord-Armee im Jahre 1813* (3 vols., Berlin, 1894), III, 225; *British and Foreign State Papers*, I, 349ff. With secret article the original of treaty is in SRA, Originaltraktater.

January, 1813, when Sweden had just expelled the French chargé; again Austria was irritated, for she was then launching her mediation plan, and wished maintenance of the *status quo*. Metternich's scheme was to make some gains by negotiation while postponing the ultimate day of reckoning. But a mediation led by Austria, ally of France, left Bernadotte cold: he had no faith in Metternich, and he knew that Norway would not be won through him or his tactics.[40]

Sweden was nevertheless vitally interested in enlisting Austria in the coalition, for her accession would give the allies both military and moral preponderance. While Neipperg was gone the indefatigable Bernadotte expatiated to chargé Binder on his interest in the reëstablishment of Austria and his determination to free Germany.[41] August Schlegel, the German nationalist, had joined the Prince, looking to him for the liberation of the German people; so Bernadotte had Schlegel write to his friends that Austria must take a stand or be crushed by either France or Russia.[42] Pressure was renewed when Neipperg returned to Stockholm from his "leave"; prospects were bright, and the Prince entertained Neipperg with dinner and two hours of optimism.[43] A few days later, braced by the fair sailing of the English negotiations, he gave Neipperg still

[40] See e.g. memorandum in Wetterstedt's hand, about April, 1813, SRA, G. L. Sam. C. S. B. Buckland, *Metternich and the British Government from 1809 to 1813* (London, 1932), is the most recent exposé of Austrian policy.

[41] K. Woynar, *Österrikes Förhållande till Sverige och Danmark . . . 1813-1814* (Stockholm, 1892), 131-133.

[42] To Sickingen, Jan. 14, 1813, intercepted by the French and now in Paris AAE, S298 (printed in Scaevola, 649-655, and other places); to Gentz, Apr. 25, Upsala, Alin Samling.

[43] Neipperg to Metternich, Feb. 16, 1813, Woynar, 141-145.

stronger assurances.   The Corsican Pozzo di Borgo,
en route from London back to the Tsar, said that he
brought British accession to the Swedish-Russian plans
for Germany, which included an invitation to Austria
to resume her supremacy, and that Britain waited im-
patiently for an Austrian declaration.   Neipperg himself seemed convinced that Austria could regain her
position only by war, but his government was super-
cautious, and was repelled both by the demands for
Norway and by the plans of Alexander for a constitutional Polish kingdom.[44]

Although disgusted with Austria's hesitancy Bernadotte continued his appeals.   Just prior to joining his
army for the campaign he sent special messages to
each of the key men in Austria.   To the Emperor he
declaimed that his army would fight for the aggrandizement of Austria and the enfranchisement of Germany;
that he wanted only Norway, in order to assure Sweden
independence; that his plan and his allies' was to repulse France to her natural frontiers for the sake of
Europe's peace, and Austrian aid was welcome; that
if fate of battle carried him to Paris he would be the
first to replace the crown on Napoleon's head, for it
would be a great evil to have a "popular system" follow a French defeat.   To archduke Charles, *"prince
de bivouac,"* he urged the reconquest of Illyria and
formation of an Italian state with the Archduke as
king, as a *"boulevard puissant contra la France."*   To
Metternich he urged that Austria resume hegemony of

[44] Neipperg to Metternich, Feb. 19, 1813, Vienna SA.  Scaevola, 658-660.
omits the Apostille, and even Woynar, 146-148, omits the final reference to
Alexander's Polish plans.

Germany and Italy; France with her natural limits was fine enough for any king; he, called to the throne of Sweden by the will of the people, limited himself to reëstablishing her safety and ancient glory. With these flattering phrases to each leader he impressed the idea that his greatest desire was an agreement with Austria.[45]

At approximately the same time an equally exalted tone was used in Vienna by Chargé Hegardt and by Knut Bildt who had been sent down from Dresden as a special envoy. Bildt's instructions struck a bold note: Carl Johan was about to appear with a respectable army to "act with energy in favor of suffering humanity." His military talents and his prestige in Europe "have raised Sweden to a degree so eminent that she can speak the language of a great power." Austria had made no definite approach to Sweden regarding her mediation scheme, yet "if the court of Vienna ranges Sweden in the class of Kingdoms whose feebleness deprives them of influence in the affairs of Europe, it is mistaken." Russia and Britain were in perfect accord with Sweden; Austrian leadership should be reëstablished; if Austria would join hands a pacification might be brought about as solid as that of Westphalia. As to the acquisition of Norway, Austria need not try to block it, for she could not prevent it; Austria and Sweden could and should be useful to each other.[46]

Nevertheless, neither in the interview with Metter-

---

[45] Binder's memorandum, Apr. 22, 1813, Woynar, 137-140. Bernadotte read this and in his round scrawl wrote, "*On a trouvé le tout très bien.*"

[46] Engeström to Bildt, Mar. 7, 17, 1813, SRA, U.S.K.; Engeström to Hegardt, Mar. 16, 19, SRA, Hegardt Bref.

nich nor in the audience with the Emperor Francis did
the Swedes get anything but suavity and fair promises.
They were told that Austria did not oppose the transfer
of Norway but only wished to avoid a Danish-Swedish
war; that the Emperor hoped for allied success but
wished to spare blood. The Swedish special mission
made no headway whatever.[47]

Vienna, as Bildt soon discovered, was a veritable
nest of anti-Swedish sentiment. Not only were the
Austrians hostile, but even the diplomats of Russia
and Prussia, allied powers, whenever the Norwegian
stipulation was mentioned,

"perdent la contenance et l'on peut presque lire sur leur
visage qu'il entre bien dans le politique de leurs souverains
de promettre des monts d'or à la Suède, mais nullement de
les donner."[48]

The only positive step Austria had taken against the
Swedish policy was an attempt by Lebzeltern, Austrian
Ambassador to Russia, to persuade Alexander to re-
strain Bernadotte from the attack on Norway. The
Austrian attitude was so obvious, however, that Sweden
saw both danger and an opportunity in the mission of
Wessenberg to London. News of the mission reached
Stockholm early, and was even in German newspapers,
yet Wessenberg traveled incognito under the name
Willmans. All went well as far as Copenhagen, where
he was received with joy. But the route to England

[47] Hegardt to Engeström, Apr. 21, 1813, SRA, Hegardt Dep.; Bildt to
Engeström, Apr. 28, SRA, Bildt Dep.

Despatches to Engeström were usually sent in duplicate to Carl Johan
after he crossed to the continent; the real Swedish foreign office followed
Carl Johan and the army.

[48] Hegardt to Engeström, May 26, 1813, SRA, Hegardt Dep.

lay through Sweden's port of Gothenburg, and Swedish
law required travelers to have government permits.
The officials were now alert, and "Willmans" and his
companion were detained while their papers were sent
to Stockholm. Here were two men bound on a mission
almost surely inimical to Swedish interests; they were
attempting to evade known Swedish law; by traveling
incognito they deprived themselves of diplomatic priv-
ileges. It gave a rare opportunity to "tweak the
mustache" of the Emperor of Austria. Crucial, too,
was this moment in early March, 1813, with the English treaty just signed; Sweden wanted no counter-
influence at work in London. Hence Wessenberg was
deliberately allowed to cool his heels. After two weeks
of most courteous entertainment by General Toll, he
was allowed to proceed; General Hope had had ample
time to get the Anglo-Swedish treaty to London.[49]

Austria can scarcely be credited with moral objections to the Norwegian claim, but she worked strenu-
ously to nullify it. Objections were stimulated by the
capable Danish Minister in Vienna, Christian Bernstorff. Probably the Austrian government wished to
preserve the strength of Denmark as a counterweight
to Prussia, and certainly she wished to maintain whatever remnants of the old order were still intact. Denmark's position, too, made her a natural proponent of

[49] Wessenberg did not charge the Swedish government with detaining
him deliberately, but on Mar. 11 Engeström wrote Löwenhielm about
Wessenberg, "on a trouvé raisonable de le faire reposer un peu à Helsing-
borg, afin que le Général Hope put arriver avant lui" (SRA, Musc.). Wessenberg's instructions are in Oncken, *Oesterreich und Preussen*, I, 416-425.
See also A. Arneth, *J. F. von Wessenberg* (2 vols., Vienna, 1898), I, 156-160;
*Gentz und Wessenberg Briefe* (Vienna and Leipzig, 1907), 63-68, 74-76,
148-160.

mediation, and thus brought her into Austria's circle.
On the other hand Vienna remembered Bernadotte as
a revolutionary ambassador, and distrusted him as a
popularly chosen ruler who symbolised the threat to
legitimacy; the Russophobe Austrians likewise knew
and feared him as the friend of the idealistic but
strangely grasping Alexander. Any aggrandizement of
Bernadotte thus chafed the already mortified self-
esteem of the Austrians. They set themselves against
his demands even before they were horrified by his bid
for the French throne.

Austria failed to thwart Sweden's policy, but Sweden
failed to gain Austrian coöperation. It was the only
big gap in Bernadotte's carefully built network of alliances. Metternich would have blasted the Prince's
hopes at the first favorable moment; Bernadotte's caution kept that moment out of history.


In his eagerness for help Carl Johan did not stop
with the larger powers. He and the Prince of Orange
discussed the possibility of forming an "Orange Legion"
to act with the Swedish forces; but this was disapproved of by the British perhaps because of "too much
Bernadotte in it."[50] With Turkey Swedish relations
are rather amusing. When the Swedish-Russian friendship was established the Swedes told the Turks how
noble and trustworthy the Russians were. In the

---

[50] The Prince of Orange visited Sweden in April, 1813, G. J. Renier,
*Great Britain and the Establishment of the Netherlands 1813-1815* (London,
1930), 74f and 84f. Perhaps the Prince of Orange feared Holland might
be offered to Denmark as compensation for Norway, as Frederick VI
thought (*Meddelelser*, VI, 303, 304).

spring of 1813, however, when the Tsar sent Dolgorouki to Copenhagen Bernadotte feared he might have to turn against Russia. He therefore ordered that Turkey be warned that Russia was near collapse, that Germany and Austria were jealous of her, and that the Finns and Poles were ready to rise against her. Fortunately the level-headed Swedish chargé in Constantinople did not follow his instructions; the incident merely illustrates the sensitiveness and the fickleness of the Swedish Prince.[51]

In the spring of 1813 Carl Johan had a network of alliances and guarantees: Britain, Russia and Prussia were snared, Austria alone had escaped him. Not until the end of the century did political morality approve the Prince's system of fore-sighted demands for specific conquest, but he knew that otherwise a small power would have to accept what was convenient. He did not enter war because of an enemy attack, or to make the world safe for anything, but because he wanted Norway—a specific territory to round out a Scandinavian kingdom; this was the price of his coöperation, his only reason for coöperation. National sentiment, a vital factor in this last drive against Napoleon both with the Prussians and with the Spaniards, had little effect among the Swedes. If active it would have called for war against Russia, the traditional enemy, for even those who wanted Norway thought to obtain it through the great Napoleon, not through a perfidious Tsar. The policy of Sweden was therefore clearly the policy of the Crown Prince, and

[51] Schinkel, *Minnen* VII, 362-364; Engeström to Palin, May 7, SRA, U.S.K.; Palin to Engeström, June 25, SRA, Turcica.

was at first opposed to the opinions of the leaders and
to the prejudices of the masses.  The Prince must win,
or his dynasty might never occupy the throne.  This
necessitated the battery of alliances and promises, and
even then Bernadotte knew that success of the "common cause" might not mean full success for him.  European sentiment was with Denmark, and Norway would
be denied him if a loophole could be found.  Caution
therefore guided all Bernadotte's movements.

# III

## INTRIGUES AND DELAYS

### *March 1813-May 1813*

AFTER Carl Johan had built his alliance support it was still many weeks before he appeared on the continent and more weeks before his army got into action. The reason for the delay was not the preliminary attack which he wished against Zealand or Norway, but a complex of misunderstandings, intrigues, suspicions.

The first difficulty was the oft-deferred transport of the Russian troops promised for a Norwegian campaign. In the winter of 1812-1813, as British agreement seemed assured, the Swedish Prince called more and more loudly for these 35,000 Russian auxiliaries.[1] But the Russians were by this time primarily concerned with the pursuit of Napoleon, and not until after the capitulation of General Yorck could Gustav Löwenhielm get a promise that the troops would actually be sent by April first (1813).[2] Even then Carl Löwenhielm from St. Petersburg warned his countrymen that the more success the Russians had the less they would do for Swedish friendship.[3]

[1] Carl Johan to C. Löwenhielm, Oct. 12 *et seq.* 1812, BFA; *Correspondance . . . Alexandre et Bernadotte . . .* , 53-55.
[2] Gustav Löwenhielm to Carl Johan, Dec. 17 *et seq.*, SRA; *Correspondance . . . Alexandre et Bernadotte . . .* , 55-56.
[3] To Engeström, Mar. 3, 5, 12, SRA, Musc.

In mid-February, 1813, Gustav Löwenhielm was sent on a new mission to the Tsar's headquarters to arrange for the transfer of the troops and to do a dozen other things suggested by his master's suspicions, imagination, and common sense. His hodge-podge instructions, jotted down from Bernadotte's dictation at intervals from February 15 to 17, told him to warn Alexander against Napoleonic and Danish intrigues, Austrian jealousy, and Prussian equivocation, to announce Bernadotte's preliminary diversion on the coasts of Pomerania, to urge Alexander to act early for the reorganization of Germany, and to emphasize the threat from an undecided Denmark. These instructions included also a unique idea: the formation of a special force of French prisoners to be attached to the allied armies and paid by Great Britain.[4] Bernadotte was already in touch with many such prisoners in Russia, and had set aside a sum for their relief. Löwenhielm was also to arrange for the control of the German Legion, a force of some 8,000 captured Germans, now to be organized and paid by Great Britain and put under Bernadotte's command.[5]

As soon as Gustav Löwenhielm reached the Russian camp a new difficulty arose to delay further the desspatch of the troops and to irritate everyone. Löwenhielm arrived on March 11, and was greeted with the

[4] "Note pour ma seconde mission en Russie 1813," in Gustav Löwenhielm's hand, SRA, G. L. Sam. The note is a mass of heterogeneous affairs, written in first, second, and third person, from Bernadotte's dictation—it, like the mission, is Bernadottian *par excellence*.

[5] Lord Cathcart, British Ambassador to Russia, at first created difficulties in this affair because of his suspicions of Bernadotte. Cathcart to Thornton, Mar. 28, 1813, Thornton to Cathcart, Apr. 12, London FO, Sweden 79.

plea that Bernadotte abandon his Norwegian campaign
and join at once the great drive against the French.
Two days later, March 13, two reports came from
Stockholm which made headquarters believe that Bernadotte intended to do exactly what they hoped. The
Russians were jubilant; now they would not have to
send Bernadotte any troops. But Löwenhielm was "as
surprised as St. John at his vision," and seemed to be
on a mission without a purpose.

The first of the misleading documents was from
Thornton to Lord Cathcart saying that since General
Hope had reached Stockholm the Swedes had accepted
as basis of negotiations with Great Britain "direct
operations on the continent against the 'common
enemy.' "[6]   Cathcart concluded naturally that the
Swedes would attack the French.   In the second document Baron Suchtelen quoted Bernadotte as saying:

"Quelles que soient les mesures à prendre relativement au
Dannemarc, il est donc arrêté, que nous nous porterons di-
rectement sur le Continent aussitôt et à mesure que m'arrive-
ront les troupes que l'Empereur m'a promises, et pour que
nous ne perdions rien de la saison, j'espére qu'on en pressera
l'expedition autant que possible.   L'acquisition de la Norvège
(continua le Prince en s'animant) ne nous arrêtera donc pas;
l'Empereur de Russie et Angleterre me la garantissent; cela
suffit, mais il faut de la celerité. . . .[7]

Strangely these despatches implying Swedish action
against the French were both written while the Swedish
and British negotiators were trying to avoid any pledge

[6] Feb. 19, 1813, London FO, Sweden 79; G. Löwenhielm to Carl Johan,
Mar. 15, SRA.
[7] Copy to C. Löwenhielm, Apr. 16, SRA, Musc.

to that effect, when all recognized that Sweden must first bring Denmark to her knees. The extravagant talk of Bernadotte, inaccurately quoted by Suchtelen, may account for one despatch, for Suchtelen insisted later that he understood the attack was to be made on the "Danish Continent," and that he omitted "Danish" only through fear of indiscreet definiteness. Thornton claimed to suppose that Cathcart knew the leeway in Hope's instructions and could interpret his statement.[8] The excuses were weak; perhaps both envoys were deceived. Yet certainly Bernadotte did not deceive them deliberately, for he was desperately eager to have the Russian auxiliaries sent him quickly, and above all he would have known that such a report would stiffen the attitude of Denmark, as it did.[9]

The natural corrective for erroneous Russian and British reports was a correct Swedish report. This was not sent, for Sweden had not changed her position since Gustav Löwenhielm left Stockholm. Why should

[8] Engeström to Löwenhielm, Apr. 13, 1813, SRA, Musc.; Engeström to Löwenhielm, Apr. 10, 17, SRA, G. L. Sam.

Bernadotte could not conceive how Cathcart could have "denatured [the conventions] to the point where they seem to be in the mind of His Imperial Majesty. These Conventions state that we will attack Femern, Fionia, Fladstrand, and the rest of the Danish continent." (Carl Johan to Gustav Löwenhielm, May 3, BFA and G. L. Sam.)

On Thornton's understanding of the treaty see *Castlereagh Corr.*, VIII, 347-348 and 376.

Neipperg wrote Metternich, (Feb. 19 and Mar. 6, 1813, Vienna SA) that Sweden intended to attack Zealand as well as Norway. Tarrach, too, on Feb. 23 wrote Goltz that the Prince held to his program, and then outlined the Prince's promises that he would come to Germany and act as the Lieutenant of the King of Prussia. This despatch also was misleading; but it was obviously only the outpouring of Bernadotte's sanguine spirit (Berlin SA, I, 20).

[9] Bernstorff to Rosenkrantz, Mar. 17, 1813, *Meddelelser*, VI, 60-61. Bernstorff got the news through Stackelberg, his Russian colleague.

he consider matters changed?    Another trouble was
that Gustav's brother Carl, the minister to Russia,
was irritated that he had been left at St. Petersburg
when the Tsar started on his campaign.  Hence, even
when the treaty with Britain was signed, March 3,
1813, no copy or explanation was sent to Count Gustav,
the only Swede at the military headquarters.  Count
Carl received a copy of the treaty but, wounded and
jealous, did not send it on to his brother.  When
Cathcart and the Tsar received the treaty, therefore,
they easily interpreted its deliberate ambiguity to mean
what they wished it to mean.  They thought it con-
firmed the earlier misleading reports.

Carl Löwenhielm at St. Petersburg heard of the misunderstanding before word reached Stockholm.  To
his brother he rushed off a protest, but still not the
treaty; to Cathcart he sent the treaty and a reminder
through the reference to the Russo-Swedish treaties,

"La réunion de la Norwège à la Suède comme base préalable
à tout cooperation de la Suède pour la Cause Commune y
est reconnue et statuée."[10]

Stockholm was still oblivious of the opinions at headquarters.  In the middle of March (1813) Carl Johan
decided voluntarily to speed his crossing.  He then
merely wrote to the Tsar and to Gustav Löwenhielm
that a Pomeranian expedition was to leave the next
day, that he would follow by April twentieth and could
accept the Russian troops on the left bank of the Oder,
and that nothing could prevent execution of "all that
has been agreed upon with His Majesty the Emperor

[10] Copies with despatches of Mar. 28-29, 1813, SRA, Musc.

Alexander." He sent no specific information about his modified campaign plans.[11]

Early in April reports from Russian headquarters at last reached Sweden, and Engeström and Carl Johan hurried off full statements of Sweden's intentions. The King held to the execution of the treaties, said Carl Johan, and the plan was to blockade the island of Zealand (including Copenhagen) and occupy the Danish continent (Holstein, Jutland), thus forcing Denmark to give up Norway. If Denmark "listened to reason" the Swedish army could advance to the Weser, the Ems, and Holland. If Alexander would send his auxiliary troops Denmark would *know* the Tsar's intentions and might yield.[12] Engeström gave a good summary of the Swedish attitude in his despatch to Gustav Löwenhielm:

"Le traité d'Alliance avec l'Angleterre fixe, il est vrai, la cooperation des troupes Suédoises sur le Continent, mais il était convenu de diriger l'attaque de manière à dévenir malgré cela directe contre le Dannemarc. Les événemens survenus dépuis ont fait juger à Monseigneur le Prince Royale qu'il pouvait employer avec avantage pour la bonne

[11] Carl Johan to G. Löwenhielm, Mar. 17, 1813, SRA, G. L. Sam.; Carl Johan to Alexander, Mar. 17, BFA. Unsatisfactory extracts in Schinkel, *Minnen*, VII, 348-349.

[12] To G. Löwenhielm, Apr. 6, 1813, SRA, G. L. Sam. G. Löwenhielm's report of Mar. 25 brought the news of misunderstanding to Stockholm; his earlier despatches of Mar. 15 and 18 were never acknowledged, yet he said they passed Stralsund and should have reached Stockholm by Apr. 1; they were not lost en route, for they now lie in Riksarkiv. (See G. Löwenhielm to Camps, Apr. 20, 1813, Upsala, Schinkel Samling VIII, and G. Löwenhielm to Carl Johan, Apr. 20, SRA. See also Morén, 241 and Schinkel, *Minnen*, VII, 357ff [incomplete]). M. Camps was a foster-brother of Bernadotte from Pau, and the Prince's most intimate companion.

Such a prolonged misunderstanding was possible only in an age of mounted couriers, boggy roads, and frail sailboats.

cause, une partie de ces forces en Allemagne. Son désir était même d'y passer avec toute l'Armée Suédoise, toujours dans la supposition que le Dannemarc céderait aux instances des trois Puissances Alliées, et que par consequent il n'aura pas laissé un ennemi sur ses derrières, qui pourrait profiter de Son absence pour attaquer la Suède."[13]

Castlereagh interpreted the Anglo-Swedish treaty exactly as did Bernadotte, and although he lamented any delay in meeting Napoleon he wrote the Prince

"If Denmark should refuse to accommodate to the general interest (which seems impossible) I trust Your Royal Highness will soon extinguish that portion of [her] military resources which is to be found in her continental provinces and which alone, whilst Seeland is blockaded, give any jealousy to your movements."[14]

To Cathcart the British foreign minister wrote that Carl Johan's right to advance on Holstein was incontrovertible, "the only question being how far Sweden can be prevailed on to relax"; Carl Johan was even entitled by treaty to be in Norway with 35,000 Russians; he must be treated with perfect fairness. Beyond cavil Bernadotte was thoroughly justified in his plan of campaign; treaties as well as military common sense demanded that Denmark join the allies or be forced to her knees.[15]

The Russians especially had no right to complain, for by now the Tsar admitted he could not fulfill his pledge of 35,000 men. Yet Alexander appealed to

[13] To G. Löwenhielm, Apr. 5, 1813, SRA, G. L. Sam.
[14] Mar. 23, 1813, copy in Apr. 13 despatch from Engeström, SRA, Musc.
[15] Hope to Castlereagh, May 21, 1813 (secret), London FO, Sweden 79; *Castlereagh Corr.*, VIII, 363-386.

Bernadotte to postpone the claims against Denmark—
appealed to his vanity, his reason, and even his cu-
pidity, saying the British could not subsidize him if
he did not fight in the common cause.[16]  And Bernadotte might have placed faith in his Russian and
British pledges if Engeström's suspicions of a great
conspiracy had not suddenly been supported by the
mission of the Russian Prince Dolgorouki to Copenhagen.

Obscurity veiled the sending of Dolgorouki, and obscurity still clouds his real purpose.  The Tsar had
made his engagements with Sweden when his empire
was in dire peril, and perhaps thought he would never
have to redeem them.  But Denmark had refused to
yield peacefully, and Bernadotte's clever forestalling
of Russian diplomacy had made compromise impossible.
During the winter the Tsar's strides toward victory
then advanced him to where Sweden was no longer an
obstacle but Denmark and Austria were.  His adviser's
hatred of Sweden and his own sympathies for Denmark, an ancient ally, were stimulated by the interest
of Austria, which sent Lebzeltern in February (1813)
to beg Alexander to restrain Bernadotte's attack.
Lebzeltern urgently stated Denmark's case—her attempts to reach agreement with Great Britain, and
her increasing military importance.  The Tsar, at first
somewhat reserved, had by March 12 told the Aus-

---

[16] Alexander to Carl Johan, Apr. 11/23, 1813, SRA, Främ.  Suv.; G.
Löwenhielm to Carl Johan, May 4, SRA.  According to the latter despatch
Alexander was still ready to make Bernadotte his generalissimo, or to give
him auxiliary troops *if* they would be used on the Elbe.

trians definitely that he regretted his obligations to
Bernadotte.[17] Then came on March 13 the false impression that Sweden would abstain from the attack
on Denmark. Why not at once draw Denmark into
the coalition? On March 14, Alexander sent Prince
Dolgorouki to Copenhagen, seemingly consulting no
one except Nesselrode.

Dolgorouki, a well-known Russian diplomat, was
much fêted after his arrival, March 22, 1813, in Copenhagen. Danish hopes were high. Yet Dolgorouki had
nothing in writing save a letter of introduction and
good-will. Rosenkrantz at last persuaded him to write
out a *Note Verbale*. Herein Denmark was told that
when King Frederick had refused Alexander's suggestion of an exchange of Norway for richer lands in
Germany the Tsar had agreed with Swedish and British representatives to postpone the question "*à un tems
plus opportun*," if Denmark would coöperate in the
cause of humanity. Denmark was invited to conquer
Holland, the Hanse cities, and the German coast region
except Hanover; she would become a power of the first
rank. Add to this Dolgorouki's oral promise that Norway would be excluded from discussion, and the Russian violation of faith is complete.[18] Reports even

[17] Mikhailowitch, *Alexandre*, II, 146-147, 152. See also Lebzeltern's
instructions. Feb. 24, 1813, Woynar, 152-154. See *Meddelelser*, VI, 60-61.
Alquier later analyzed, probably correctly, that Austrian pressure induced
the Tsar to abandon Sweden but that Bernadotte then intimidated him
and brought him back to his obligations (to Bassano, May 24, Paris AAE,
D187).

[18] Holm, *Danske Magazin*, VI R., II B., 66, dated Mar. 25, 1813. See
also Morén, 195; Alexander to Frederick, Mar. 2/14, 1813, DRA, Forestillinger; *Meddelelser*, VII, 40. Morén (187-204) has the best account of the
Dolgorouki mission as a whole, although he did not know the documents
in Mikhailowitch's *Alexandre*.

claimed that Alexander had said he would not lend
Bernadotte a single soldier and that 35,000 would make
him too powerful in Germany.[19]  Such startling treachery forces one to consider the possibility that Dolgorouki surpassed his instructions; on the matter of
Norway perhaps he did, but otherwise the whole offer
sounds surprisingly like that made to Blome the previous November.  It must be remembered that the envoy
was sent the day after Alexander thought he had
learned that Bernadotte was coming immediately to
Germany.  Thus it may indicate that Alexander realized he would be safe from Swedish retaliation once
Bernadotte and his army were on the continent, and
it may indicate the fate of the Norwegian claim if
Bernadotte had allowed himself thus to get caught.
The secrecy of the move further strengthens the cir-
cumstantial evidence against it.

The Danes were optimistic, exaggerating the British
desire for peace, and their own strategic position.
Frederick VI took a commanding tone in his reply to
the *Note Verbale*.  He demanded that when Danish
troops should join the allies the Tsar should guarantee
the integrity of all Danish territory, especially Norway; coöperation must be conditioned upon peace with
Great Britain, which meant in turn freedom of commerce, restoration of Danish colonies, and restoration
of or compensation for the fleet and naval stores taken
in 1807.[20]  Count Moltke took this reply to the Tsar,

[19] Camps to G. Löwenhielm, Apr. 17, 1813, SRA, G. L. Sam.; *Castlereagh
Corr.*, VIII, 382ff.

[20] Mar. 27, 1813 (draft), DRA, Forestillinger.  A note from the king is
"entirely approving" (Holm, *Danske Magazin*, VI R., II B., 1 hft., 67ff),
and see also *Meddelelser*, VI, 84-85, 113-114.

while direct to London was sent Count Bernstorff, hope reborn despite the failure of Bille.

Pro-Russian sentiment grew in Copenhagen, and insults were heaped upon Alquier and other Frenchmen.[21] But Swedish troops had landed in Pomerania, and the Danes had still to prove their friendship with Russia. Hence Rosenkrantz persuaded his King to occupy Hamburg, Lübeck, and Travemünde, on condition the Swedes be excluded therefrom. General Tettenborn, however, dared not admit the Danes on such a condition—much to the relief of the Hamburgers, who feared Danish control.[22] Dolgorouki's appeal to Tettenborn was fruitless, and convinced the trustful Danes that there was something wrong.[23] Dolgorouki's plan was, of course, to get the Danes irretrievably entangled against France.

The Swedes were now aroused. They feared that this proposed occupation was a scheme of the Danes to get control of the cities, and then turn them over to France. They began to realize the other dangers of Dolgorouki's intrigue when Baudissin asked Thornton why Britain wished Norway to go to Sweden when Russia was not at all interested in this.[24] The Swedish chargé in Copenhagen, Lorichs, seemed blind to trouble, but when Dolgorouki read him his *Note Verbale* (and

[21] Alquier to Bassano, May 16, 1813, and Devear to Bassano, May 23 Paris AAE, D187. Reports that Bernadotte had given up the Norway claim reached Copenhagen *via* Vienna and Berlin (*Meddelelser*, VI, 121, 122).

[22] *Meddelelser*, VI, 122-125, 183-187; Sørensen, *Kampen*, I, 97, 113-114.

[23] Dolgorouki to Tettenborn, Apr. 10, 14, 20, 1813, (copies to G. Löwenhielm, May 9, SRA, G. L. Sam.).

[24] Engeström to Rehausen, Apr. 19, 1813, SRA, Anglica; to G. Löwenhielm, Apr. 5, SRA, G. L. Sam.

why did he do so?) the summary of it dismayed
Engeström. Lorichs was at once replaced by the
young secretary, Hochschild, who was ordered to get
to the bottom of things. To him Dolgorouki insisted
that both Cathcart and Gustav Löwenhielm had agreed
to postpone the question of Norway. Either he lied
or was himself deceived. Hochschild thought he had
exceeded instructions in giving a written note, but
that his propositions conformed to the Tsar's intentions; Hochschild had "always believed that the Russian government forgot easily through success."[25]

Policy made Carl Johan insist that Dolgorouki must
have violated the instructions of Alexander, but his
distrust was deep. Protests were speeded to the Tsar,
and with them the demand that Russia break off
diplomatic relations with Denmark. Cold suspicion
and leashed anger spoke in Carl Johan's next letter to
Gustav Löwenhielm, and he asked, what if Sweden
had attacked Russia in 1812 along with France, Turkey
and Persia? Yet he reiterated faith in the Tsar, and
said it was for him to say whether the Swedish attack
should be delivered in Holstein or in Zealand, but in
either case he should furnish the 35,000 men.[26] After
a few days to calm himself Bernadotte wrote direct to
Alexander:

". . . je suis très chagrin de l'effet qu'a produit la manière
dont le Prince Dolgorouki a rempli sa mission. Suivant
lui V.M. l'interesse vivement au Danemarc et très peu à la
Suède. Accoutumé à mille changemens dans la suite des

[25] Hochschild and Lorichs to Engeström, Mar. 31, Apr. 12, 1813, SRA,
Danica.
[26] Apr. 11, 1813, SRA, G. L. Sam.

affaires et des événemens mon âme s'était fortement trompée
à l'école de l'adversité et de la fortune; mon esprit et ma
raison me représentaient tout chanceux dans cette vie, mais
nos traités avec V.M. avaient acquis un tel caractère de
foi auprès de moi, que je suis entrainé à professer un espèce
de culte, non seulement pour ces mêmes traités, mais encore
pour les paroles prononcées par V.M. Excusez, Sire, la
sensibilité dont cette lettre porte l'empreinte; je n'y trace
que foiblement mon emotion. Puisse-t-elle renouveller à
V.M. la conviction de l'attachement vrai que je lui porterai
toujours. Vous dire, Sire, que j'ai besoin que ma politique
et mon coeur soient rassurés sur les resolutions que prendra
V.M., c'est dire que pour exister j'ai besoin de l'air que je
respire."[27]

Before these protests reached the Russian headquarters Nesselrode had written Dolgorouki to try
once more to convince Frederick VI that although
Norway must be sacrificed the compensation would be
ample,[28] and Alexander had told Löwenhielm that the
mission showed little hope and that he had ordered
Dolgorouki to leave Copenhagen if the King did not
decide quickly.[29] These items are the best evidence
available of Russian good faith, but they are scarcely
proof. In any case Dolgorouki's mission failed because
his arrangements could not be made quickly or quietly
enough. When the Swedish explanations of the treaty
with Britain and the Swedish protests against Dolgorouki reached headquarters the Tsar, though bitterly
disappointed, immediately disavowed his agent and

[27] Apr. 17, 1813, BFA.
[28] Copy with Rosenkrantz to Moltke, Apr. 22, DRA, Dolgorouki.
[29] G. Löwenhielm to Carl Johan, Apr. 15, 1813, SRA.

ordered him to Berlin, condemning his "unreflecting conduct."[30]

Moltke, meanwhile, was rusticating at the Tsar's headquarters. He had to wait three days to see Alexander, then was told that the Danish offer of 10,000 troops could not be discussed until Denmark ceded Norway. He begged that Russia send grain to starving Norway, and surreptitious commerce soon developed. He was told that Denmark must inevitably lose Norway, and the only wise course was to make an agreement with the allies to gain compensation in Germany. Moltke saw, however, the Russian antipathy toward the whole affair, so lingered on in hopeful desperation. But treaties and gratitude, and perhaps fear of the impulsive Gascon, kept Alexander true to his first bargain. In negotiating peace with Great Britain through Lord Cathcart Moltke had no better success. Cathcart was as sympathetic as were the Russian officers, and as powerless. Since Denmark would not even promise a breach with France for acceptance of her high demands, there was nothing to negotiate. Even when the Danish terms were lowered to an abject appeal for peace it was hopeless, though Moltke persisted until mid-June.[31] Count Bernstorff, who was sent to London to negotiate directly, fared even worse than Moltke, for he was not

[30] G. Löwenhielm to Carl Johan, Apr. 20, 27, 1813, SRA; Alexander to Carl Johan, Apr. 17/29, Apr. 19/May 1, May 12/24, SRA, Främ. Suv.; Nesselrode to Suchtelen, Apr. 15/27 (copy with Wetterstedt to Rehausen, May 9, SRA, Anglica); *Meddelelser*, VI, 134-136. The condemnation of Dolgorouki was more for his "indiscretion" than for his offers.

[31] DRA, Dolgorouki (extracts in *Meddelelser*, VI, 173-178). Moltke could not treat with the Tsar unless, and until, he could gain assurances of British coöperation from Cathcart; Morén (264ff) minimizes the British angle of the mission, I think unduly.

allowed so much as to stay to await a shift in the diplomatic breeze.

When Dolgorouki announced his disavowal Rosenkrantz is said to have exclaimed, "You have ruined us! On the faith of your words we have gone so far with Russia that Napoleon will never pardon us."[32] The Swedes were almost as depressed as the Danes, for they saw their "noble restraint" of 1812 repaid by traditional Russian perfidy. Russophobia was rearoused, and Bernadotte considered abandoning the alliance and acting independently against Denmark.[33] With a glance backward to Charles XII and Peter he reminded the Tsar that the Swedish army "still remembers Narva, and it is not now sunk in the deserts of Ukraine."[34] As already noted he tried to prepare Turkey for an attack on Russia, and he warned the King of Prussia against the Tsar.[35]

The structure of mutual confidence among the allies was repaired, but was never the same again. The Dolgorouki incident plus the misunderstandings about the Russian auxiliaries and the Anglo-Swedish treaty delayed the Swedish forces. Meantime disappointed Denmark was forced definitely back into Napoleon's arms. The Dolgorouki incident had been a double catastrophe for the allies.

[32] Hochschild to Engeström, Apr. 23, 1813, SRA, Danica. See Prince Christian Frederik to Kaas, Apr. 23, DRA, Kaas Privat Arkiv.

[33] Camps to G. Löwenhielm, Apr. 17, 1813, Carl Johan and Wetterstedt to G. Löwenhielm, May 9, SRA, G. L. Sam.; Engeström to Rehausen, May 5, SRA, Anglica; Neipperg to Metternich, Apr. 17, Vienna SA.

[34] To G. Löwenhielm, May 3, 1813, SRA, G. L. Sam.

[35] To Frederick William, May 3, 1813, BFA.

Sweden's attempts to threaten or cajole Denmark into a peaceful solution had failed miserably. Just as unsuccessful were her schemes for arousing Norway to rise and demand union with Sweden. Count Wedel-Jarlsberg headed a small party of Norwegians who favored such a union because of their hatred of the Danes, who for centuries had neglected and robbed the northern kingdom. Nevertheless the masses of the people hated the proud Swedes even more, so that the work of Wedel-Jarlsberg and the Swedish agents scattered about Norway bore almost no fruit. Even in the face of famine the people trusted the promises of Frederick VI and would not be bribed by offers of Swedish grain.[36]

Carl Johan was desperately anxious for a quick settlement of his claims to Norway, and continued to the last moment his persistent but basically unchanging proposals. Count Stedingk was called upon to plead with Denmark Sweden's geographic "right" to Norway, but Rosenkrantz merely ridiculed the idea.[37] On March 30, 1813, the Swedes learned of the brief armistices the Danes had won with Russia and Britain by misrepresenting their peace negotiations; worried anew, Bernadotte threatened to attack Denmark between April 15 and 20 if she had not then joined the allies, for he dared not advance an army while an unregenerate Denmark and Norway endangered his rear. Wetterstedt would negotiate an agreement in Copenhagen if King Frederick would cede Trondhjem and the two

[36] Morén, 208-209; *Meddelelser*, VI, 298-307; spy reports from Norway in Stockholm KB, Engeström Sam.

[37] Rosenkrantz to Stedingk, Apr. 10, 1813, SRA, Snör.

forts of Kongsvinger and Fredrikshald; the rest of
Norway Denmark might retain even after the general
peace if she would yield Sweden her German indemnities. If Denmark did not agree she would be iso-
lated, the only state not coöperating in the European
cause. Hochschild was to explain when he presented
these terms how much Sweden needed Norway, and
how excellent were her military resources and her
credit.[38]

The Danes refused the proposals with hauteur and
a certain confidence (April 10), for Dolgorouki had
raised their hopes and they had just decided to coöperate with the Russians at Hamburg. Danish skies
again quickly darkened when this coöperation was refused, and when Thornton assured Baudissin anew
that Britain was at one with Sweden.[39] Rosenkrantz,
with self-confidence shattered but hope still alive,
asked Thornton at last for negotiations on the sole
basis of Danish-Norwegian territorial integrity.[40] It
was too late.

When a Danish gunboat cut some cables on the
Swedish shore the Stockholm government issued a
warning that future trespassers would be sunk. A
few days later the Kronborg (Elsinore) fort fired on
some Swedish vessels guarding a British convoy
through the Sound. On April 16, 1813, Sweden sent

[38] Schinkel, *Minnen, Bihang*, III, 142-144; Engeström to Lorichs, Apr.
1, 6, 1813, SRA, Danica; instructions for Hochschild, Apr. 1, SRA, U.S.K.

[39] Lorichs to Engeström, Apr. 9, 12, 1813, and Hochschild to Engeström,
Apr. 9, SRA, Danica; Anker-Wrangel, 210-213; Most of the official Danish
reply is in Nielsen, *Aktmaessige Bidrag . . . 1812-1813* (Christiania, 1876),
34f.

[40] Anker-Wrangel, 214-216; Engeström to Hochschild, Apr. 16, 18,
SRA, U.S.K.

her real ultimatum: the officer responsible for the firing must be courtmartialed in six days or Sweden would break diplomatic relations.  Two alternative settlements were proposed with the ultimatum: (1) for immediate possession of Trondhjem and of the two forts (or their demolition) Sweden would wait for the rest of Norway until the French were pushed beyond the Rhine and compensation won for Denmark by a Swedish-Danish army; (2) for immediate possession of all Norway Sweden would relinquish 1,000,000 riksdalers of claims against Denmark, pay 2,000,000 riksdalers, cede Pomerania to Denmark, and keep her army on the continent until Denmark had full territorial compensation.[41]

Rosenkrantz received the ultimatum on April 21 and the King decided to conduct the courtmartial as a means of staving off war.[42]  But the Swedes had decided to chance no trickery, and on the heels of the ultimatum (April 22) came the recall of Hochschild and the expulsion of Baudissin.  Bitterly Rosenkrantz said that the courtmartial was now useless.[43]  The Danes were agonized.  Dolgorouki was pitiful, sure now of disavowal.  The government appealed anew to Austria, but prices of Swedish goods soared and Denmark was regarded as lost.[44]

[41] Engeström to Hochschild, Apr. 16, SRA, U.S.K.; Anker-Wrangel, 215.
[42] *Meddelelser*, VII, 44-45, 45-46.
[43] *Meddelelser*, VI, 128; Hochschild to Engeström, Apr. 23, SRA, Danica; Engeström to Hochschild, Apr. 18, SRA, U.S.K.
[44] Rosenkrantz to Engeström, Apr. 24, 1813, Stockholm KB, Engeström Samling; Hochschild to Engeström, Apr. 23, 25, 27, SRA, Danica; *Meddelelser*, VI, 129, 130-131.

The Swedish General Sandels had meanwhile reoccupied Pomerania, thus tapping important grain supplies and forestalling a Russian occupation of this area evacuated by the French. But Bernadotte, even after the breach with Denmark, lingered almost four weeks in Sweden. Many factors are required to explain the delay: transport difficulties, time-consuming preparations, non-arrival of the Russian troops, suspicions of the Dolgorouki mission and of the Danish attempts to join the coalition. This delay and the *impasse* in Swedish-Danish relations exasperated Sweden's allies almost beyond endurance.

The Prince Regent of England wrote Carl Johan that early action in Germany was the only purpose of the treaty of March third; Castlereagh admitted Sweden's right to attack Denmark but finally begged that the attack be abandoned, for it endangered parliamentary approval of the subsidy. Liverpool added his appeal; the commercial house handling the subsidy grew anxious; Rehausen feared that the publication of the treaty would cause the fall of the Ministry unless Bernadotte acted against the "common enemy." General Hope was sent out anew to impress Bernadotte "in the strongest manner" with British impatience.[45]

German exasperation reached a high pitch. Kotzebue wrote in the *Russisches und Deutsches Volksblatt*,

---

[45] Prince Regent to Carl Johan, Mar. 27, 1813, SRA, Främ. Suv.; Rehausen to Carl Johan, Mar. 23, SRA, C. J. Papper 88; Rehausen's despatches Apr. 30 to May 25, SRA, Anglica; Cooke to Hope, May 26, London FO, Sweden 79.

"les suédois sont lents: ils ont 600 hommes à Rostock et
600 hommes en Poméranie, mais ils ne font rien; ils disent
qu'ils n'ont pas d'ordre."[46]

The Countess of Pappenheim flattered the Prince and
pled with him to be the hero and leader of Germany;
with "vast impatience" she awaited him.[47]  The Prussian Minister Goltz wanted the British Colonel Cooke
to help him force Bernadotte to renounce his preliminary campaign against Denmark.  He sensed that the
Swedes felt uncertain of allied support and that their
army was in Germany not so much to fight the French
as "to make the Danes more tractable."[48]  King Frederick William argued that action in Germany would
best further Bernadotte's own schemes, and eventually
granted Bülow's corps to the Prince, *"dans la supposition que vous pousserez le plutôt vos troupes en avant."*[49]

Tsar Alexander did not fulfill his own obligations but
he sent the rabid Napoleon-hater Pozzo di Borgo to
urge Sweden to surpass her obligations.  Pozzo waited
day after day in Carlscrona while the Prince took a
slow inspection tour in Sweden.  Bernadotte's Gascon
blood had boiled when he heard rumors that Russia
"had no more need of Sweden" and might repudiate
agreements now "inoperative."  Even Wetterstedt had
become excited when the Tsar wrote that he would
send the troops agreed upon *if* Bernadotte "will act

[46] G. Löwenhielm to Carl Johan, May 4, 1813, SRA.

[47] Schinkel, *Minnen*, VII, 369-372.

[48] Goltz to Hardenberg, Apr. 28, 1813, to Frederick William, May 9,
Hardenberg to Goltz, May 3 (draft), Berlin SA, Nor.  As the Prussians
thought, the Swedes had orders to do nothing until Bernadotte arrived.

[49] To Carl Johan, May 23, 27, 1813, SRA, Främ. Suv.

immediately against France." Both Wetterstedt and
the Prince's confidant, Camps, said that if Russia did
not send the troops and break relations with Denmark
Sweden would have to retire; the Prince wrote Engeström to prepare the way for anti-Russian action.[50]

When Bernadotte at last reached Carlscrona he was
partly placated by the Tsar's disavowal of Dolgorouki,
but angered anew by the absence of the Russian troops.
He received the Corsican Pozzo at midnight, and with
rapier-like tongues the two battled the night through.
Bernadotte digressed heatedly on military honor,
Swedish national feeling, Napoleon, and struck fire on
the fulfillment of treaties, the Dolgorouki mission, and
his need for Norway. Pozzo, who boasted to the Tsar
of his merciless frankness, insisted that the Russian
guarantee of Norway was inviolable, but that the
method of obtaining it must depend on circumstances,
not on the *"lettre morte des traités."* The strength of
his argument was that Bernadotte's acquisition of
Norway really depended on the success of the "common cause." The angry debaters separated only as
the morning sun streamed in. However Bernadotte
might feel, 15,000 Swedish soldiers were already in
Germany; he must proceed or retire. In the afternoon
he announced that he would proceed—with reservations: he would cross the Baltic and send a small
detachment for observation only as far as the Elbe;
he still demanded the Russian troops and a decision

---

[50] Alexander to Carl Johan, Apr. 11/23, 1813, SRA, Främ. Suv.; Wetterstedt to Engeström, May 11, SRA; Camps to G. Löwenhielm, May 9,
SRA, G. L. Sam.; see above, p. 45.

from Denmark before he would lead his army against Napoleon.[51]

As late as April 6 Bernadotte had planned an advance into Holstein and Schleswig with Swedish, Russian and German troops. What he visioned then with eager energy was postponed and embittered by the intrigues and delays but still more by the weather. Swedish ships were insufficient, but had transported 15,000 men. The British ships to carry the rest were held back by uncommonly contrary winds and beaten by storms until they were a full month late at Carlscrona.[52] Against such a conspiracy of nature man's sails were helpless.

Bernadotte landed at Stralsund on May 18, to be met by scores of appeals to be the "savior hero" of Germany. Berlin had been frightened by a French threat and hundreds had left the city; the Swedish chargé had burned his archives. Davoust was advancing on pro-ally Hamburg, threatening to wreak vengeance and to bottle up Germany's leading commercial and financial center and her only port in direct communication with London. Letters and committees and Bernadotte's own eager officers urged immediate aid to Tettenborn and his Cossacks who could not alone hold the city.[53]

[51] Wetterstedt to Engeström, May 8, 1813, SRA; Pozzo to Suchtelen, Apr. 26/May 8, Upsala, Alin Samling XII.

[52] Carl Johan to Admiral Puke, Mar. 30, Apr. 3, 1813, to Sandels, Apr. 6, 10, BFA; Wetterstedt to Rehausen, May 11, 13, 19, SRA, Anglica; Hope to Castlereagh, May 14, London FO, Sweden 79.

[53] Adlercreutz to Engeström, Apr. 29, 1813, Stockholm KB, Engeström Samling; Alopeus to Carl Johan, May 5/17 (copy), SRA, G. L. Sam.; Suremain, *Mémoires*, 277ff; Palmstierna (chargé in Berlin) to Engeström, May 16, 21, SRA, Borus.; Alexander to Carl Johan, May 12/24, SRA,

The impatient and humiliated Swedes were held in leash by a leader as cautious in action as he was impulsive in speech. Even the transports were retained for the withdrawal of troops in case Russia and Prussia did not send their long overdue detachments.[54] The Prussians had not ratified the April treaty and obviously hoped they would not have to do so once Sweden became irrevocably involved in their cause. Bernadotte thus lacked both material and moral support from his allies, and at the very moment when their lines were withdrawing after their check at Lutzen (May 3). Denmark, furthermore, could easily and joyfully surround and put *hors de combat* any force the Swedes might throw into Hamburg.[55] When he saw conditions on the continent Bernadotte did agree to use Russian and Prussian forces against the French unless Denmark attacked him, and he repeated his offers to Denmark.[56] On the other hand he complained of Russian hedging, of the omission of Sweden from the convention of Breslau (on the reorganization of Germany), and asserted that if Denmark was allowed to coöperate before accepting Swedish terms he would "by this fact

Främ. Suv.; Engeström, *Minnen*, II, 349-350; Goltz to Frederick William, May 14, Berlin SA, I, 20; Schück, *Excellensen Grefve A. F. Skjöldebrands Memoarer* (5 vols., Stockholm, 1904), V, 8-9; T. T. Hojer, "En Hanseatisk Karl Johansbeundrare på försommare 1813," *Historisk Tidskrift* (1934), 186-190.

[54] Especially: Carl Johan to Admiral Puke, May 27, 1813, BFA; Hope to Castlereagh, May 21, London FO, Sweden 79.

[55] The best thing on the military situation at Hamburg is Tingsten, *Huvuddragen . . . 1809-1813*, 165-178. Oncken is unfair and inaccurate (*Oesterreich und Preussen*, II, 418). See also Quistorp, *Geschichte der Nord Armee im Jahre 1813* (3 vols., Berlin, 1894).

[56] Dictated to Pozzo di Borgo, May 19, 1813 (copies in SRA, G. L. Sam. XII).

be delivered from all that his eagerness to be useful to the general cause has dictated. . . ."[57]

The force which was sent in advance to the Elbe caused extreme embarrassment, for General Döbeln disobeyed orders and sent four battalions into Hamburg. The Swedes thought honor was retrieved and the Hamburgers hailed Bernadotte as their savior. But the Prince was angered by the disobedience and the possible upset of political plans. Immediately he sent General Lagerbring to displace Döbeln and withdraw the troops; the new instructions closed with:

"Le G<sup>al</sup> Lagerbring est instruit que mon intention est de ne pas combattre jusqu'à ce que les Russes et les Prussiens m'ayant joint, et que jusqu'à cette époque le volonté irrévocable du Roi est que je ne m'occupe que de la défense des frontières de la Poméranie. Le G<sup>al</sup> Lagerbring a donc à se régler dans ses mouvemens sur la connaissance que je lui donne de la politique du Roi et de ses projets ultérieures."[58]

Further instructions next day remarked that ever since Charles XII Swedish soldiers had fought well but with sad results; now a new era should begin, but the first essential was discipline. In any case a city could better be defended on its lines of communication than in its streets. A characteristic warning was added: "Mistrust everyone and above all the Danes. The metamorphoses of governments in our time should remind us constantly of the old adage: honor to the

[57] Carl Johan to Alexander, May 21, 1813, BFA. Schinkel prints this, but through his generous courtesy omits the paragraph with the threat! (*Minnen*, VII, 377-381).

[58] Carl Johan to Lagerbring, May 21, 1813, BFA.

strong."[59]   On May 26 the Swedes left Hamburg, to
the despair of the city and the angry disappointment
of the allies.

Bernadotte evidently hoped only to threaten France
while he brought Denmark to terms, and probably he
hoped he might not have to fight at all; he wrote once
that he came to the continent to contribute "*à la paix
générale et de combattre pour cette noble cause s'il le
fallait.*"[60]   He was no longer merely a general, he was
a prince responsible for the policy of a state, and if he
could achieve the aims of the state without war so
much the better.   As for Hamburg, his policy was wise
from the broad military standpoint, even the British
General Hope writing of "the mad Swedish General
who led the corps into Hamburg."[61]   When the Russians withdrew from Hamburg King Frederick had at
last decided to occupy it.   Danes entered to hold it
against either French or Swedes, but when Bernstorff
was rebuffed in London Frederick then decided to hold
the city for Napoleon.   His orders were disobeyed,
however, prior to Döbeln's entry; the Danish troops
evacuated on May 19.   The Swedes entered on the
twenty-first.   Hence by sheer luck there was no clash
at Hamburg.[62]   Financially and morally disastrous as
was the loss of the city to the advancing French, the
loss was probably inevitable, especially after the second

[59] To Lagerbring, May 22, 1813, BFA.   Schinkel of course omits the
slur on Swedish discipline (*Minnen*, VII, 382).

[60] To Lagerbring, May 26, 1813, Stockholm BFA.   This too is garbled
in the *Recueil des Ordres de Mouvement* . . . (Stockholm, 1839), 21, and
worse by Schinkel (*Minnen*, VII, 384).

[61] Hope to Castlereagh, May 21, 22 (two), 1813, London FO, Sweden 79.

[62] Tingsten, *op. cit.*, 161-164; *Meddelelser*, VI, 182-297.

allied defeat at Bautzen, May 20-21. Fortunate indeed were the allies that Bernadotte's small force was not caught in that advanced outpost.

When Denmark was forced to return in humiliation to the Napoleonic fold the King sent President of the Chancellery Kaas with a humble apology to the Emperor. Tettenborn suggested that Kaas might listen to conciliatory Swedish propositions, and in the period of depressed hopes Carl Johan ordered General Boye to interview him. The proposition still demanded Trondhjem but omitted the forts, gave Denmark a chance to choose between German indemnities and southern Norway at the peace, and was accompanied by a warning against Napoleon's wrath, assurances of Danish expansion and renewed commerce if she would join the allies. Boye missed President Kaas, took the offer to Colonel Haffner at Altona, then to Hamburg and to Lübeck. It was useless.[63]

A direct appeal to Copenhagen was likewise attempted, on the suggestion of General Hope and Thornton. They and Wetterstedt, with Suchtelen along as "unofficial observer," sailed in the British ship *Defiance* to Kioge Bay outside Copenhagen. The appealing notes they sent in to Rosenkrantz left the terms unchanged, and the Danes sent a prompt rejection direct to the vessel; the envoys did not land.

[63] Kaas' reports are in DRA, Kaas Privat Arkiv; Tettenborn to Carl Johan, May 22 (copy), SRA, Anglica; Wetterstedt to Rehausen, May 28, SRA, Anglica; Carl Johan to Boye, May 30, BFA; Stierneld to Engeström, June 2, SRA. And see Kaas, *Frederik den Sjettes Udsoning Med Napoleon* (Copenhagen, 1894).

It was at this moment, May 21, that Col. Peyron reached Hamburg with Napoleon's latest offer to Sweden (see below, ch. vii).

What had saddened the sanguine Gascon had stiffened the stubborn Dane.[64]

Was Bernadotte sincere in these final offers of reconciliation? The offer to accept only Trondhjem seemed to relinquish the very essence of his program. One cannot but suspect that he counted upon border disputes or revolt in Norway to enable him later to conquer what he was not then demanding. Or did he make concessions only to humor the English, knowing any offer would be rejected? Or did he want to make any possible settlement so as to have his hands free to pursue projects in France? Or is the obvious explanation the true one—that his suspicions of his allies made him ready to accept gratefully whatever he could get?

Up to the first of June Bernadotte kept demanding the Russian and Prussian troops, and he clung to the Holstein campaign as the most he could do to compromise between his own goal and the "common cause." On June first he wrote Rehausen that he would retire to Sweden if the allies did not keep their promises.[65] He talked wildly of how Alexander had betrayed him and Frederick William wished to betray him, of how they had used his women friends to excite his ambitions, and had proposed him for Emperor of France; but, he exclaimed, he had not fallen into their trap, he would rather have a retreat in Lapland than rule over

[64] Hope and Thornton to Castlereagh, May 28, 1813, London FO, Sweden 78; *Meddelelser*, VI, 178-181, 423-424. See also Forssell, *Wetterstedt*, 178-185.

[65] Scaevola, 358-362 and Schinkel, *Minnen*, *Bihang*, III, 154-158; also Carl Johan to Woronzov, June 1, BFA.

a degraded people—"and the French are degraded."[66]
Soon after the first of June, however, his spirits rose.
He had received word from Wallmoden and Bülow
that they and their corps had been attached to his
army.  He saw that within two weeks he might have
an army of 100,000 men, and wrote Wallmoden,

"Dès ce moment l'issue de la campagne est décidée et
l'equilibre de l'Europe assuré; mais tout que les traités
n'auront pas obtenu leur exécution, le sort de l'Alliance me
parait incertain."[67]

He ordered all communication between Denmark and
Norway cut, and on June 7 wrote that he waited only
for Gustav Löwenhielm's return to decide when to
begin the attack.[68]  All obstacles had been overcome;
at last everything was ready for the great offensive.

[66] Suremain, 288f (May 28, 1813).
[67] June 3, 1813, BFA.
[68] To Woronzov, etc., June 5, 7, 1813, BFA.  Wetterstedt emphasized
that as soon as Carl Johan had 15,000 allied troops he would advance,
sure of their good intentions; he did not promise that the advance would
be directly against Napoleon, as Forssell claims (in his *Wetterstedt*, 187).

## IV

### The Armistice and Plan of Campaign

*June to August 1813*

THE Swedish troops were collected, the allies' auxiliaries were being put under Bernadotte's orders, Denmark had taken a hostile position—the Crown Prince of Sweden was ready to act. Then, on June 4, Russia and Prussia signed an armistice with Napoleon. The allies needed time to consolidate their gains, collect troops, and get slow-moving Austria into the coalition; Napoleon needed time for the same purposes. Technically the armistice did not include the British or the Swedes, but practically it did, for the British had no troops and it would have been suicide for 30,000 Swedes to fight France single-handed. A respite may have been essential for military and political reasons, but the news of it which reached Stralsund on June 9 created consternation and annihilated plans for advance.

Bernadotte kept Löwenhielm at Russian headquarters to guard Swedish interests in case of a peace conference, but he pled for war. He sent General Skjöldebrand to the Tsar with three possible plans of campaign and a warning that to allow Napoleon to dictate peace would be to dig a grave for Europe. He reminded the Tsar of his high duty—"he belonged not only to Russia but to the world," and suggested a conference between Tsar, King and Prince.[1]  Bernadotte was eager for renewal of the war because of the embarrassing and really critical position in which he was placed by the long inactivity.

The first and greatest anxiety concerned relations with Denmark and Norway.  Swedish policy had of course angered Denmark but had not yet brought her to declare war.  In case the armistice led to a general peace Bernadotte could hardly hope to gain Norway, for he had so far accomplished nothing; his whole program would be a huge fiasco, and he would return to Sweden with an embittered Denmark awaiting an opportunity for revenge.  As to Norway itself the situation looked bad, for Christian Frederick, heir to the Danish throne, had slipped into Norway and was arousing the people against Sweden.  Swedish spies reported that Norway would join Sweden only if forced by hunger or the sword.  Bernadotte did not falter; he would do what Carl X and Carl XI had failed to do; he would make Sweden once more a power.[2]  To do so, however, he must have war with Denmark, and he set about to goad her into a declaration.  On June 15 he ordered that Swedish boats refuse to pay the Sound dues, and that all Danes at Carlscrona be

[1] Wetterstedt to Engeström, June 11, 1813, SRA; Carl Johan to G. Löwenhielm, June 11, and Wetterstedt to G. Löwenhielm, June 13, 14, SRA, G. L. Sam.; Carl Johan to Alexander, June 11, BFA (incomplete in Schinkel, *Minnen*, VII, 395ff).

[2] Essen to Wetterstedt, May 16, 1813, SRA, Danmark-Norge 5; reports on Norway from Rosen, Eckstedt, Adlersparre, Edman, Essen, and Rahmn, Stockholm KB, Engeström Samling; Carl Johan to Essen and to Carl XIII, June 21, BFA.

arrested as spies; on June 25 he ordered the blockade of the Danish fleet.[3]

Sweden could hardly rely on her own strength alone, however, in a contest with Denmark. Therefore Britain was invited, in case of a continental peace, to join Sweden in a separate attack on Denmark. For her aid Britain would gain the island of Zealand as a depot for commerce, and a "new Gibraltar" of the Baltic. Oncken calls this scheme one of the Gascon's *luftschlössern*, yet Castlereagh gave it conditional approval at once, and when the Prince definitely resigned his own claims to Zealand Count Münster gained Castlereagh's full approbation.[4] The far-sighted Crown Prince had retained the British transports. Now, if war was resumed he could advance into Germany, and if peace was signed by Russia and Prussia he could attack Denmark with British naval support. Once again Bernadotte had adapted his policy to the needs of the moment.

The high-handed attitude of Russia and Prussia regarding the reorganization of Germany also angered Bernadotte although it did not actually endanger his position. Here again the Prince was able to shift from his former coöperation with Alexander to a more satisfactory coöperation with Great Britain. Swedish interest in Pomerania and British interest in Hanover both demanded the curtailment of Stein's great ambitions for Prussian expansion. Although Bernadotte

[3] To Carl XIII, Toll, and Puke, June 15, 25, 1813, BFA.

[4] Oncken, *Oesterreich und Preussen*, II, 419-421; Wetterstedt to Rehausen, June 20, 30, 1813, Rehausen to Wetterstedt, July 6, 9, 23, SRA, Anglica; *Castlereagh Corr.*, VIII, 399-402, 402-404; Foreign Office draft to Hope, June 17, London FO, Sweden 79.

at first exaggerated British concern about George III's
holdings in Germany he found Hanover's Count
Münster an able and useful ally to have in London.[5]
Bernadotte's successful administration of Hanover in
1804-1805 increased his sympathy for its enlargement
into a great Guelph state, and likewise laid the foundation for the suggestion that he become *Statholder* for
the Hanse cities.[6]

For these reasons as well as because of Swedish de-
pendence on British subsidies, naval support and commercial relations, the policy of the two states grew
increasingly closer in the summer of 1813.   Stein's
policy of enlargement of Prussia had gained headway
as the Russian armies moved westward and his influence was evident in the Convention of Breslau (Mar.
7/19, 1813) by which the Tsar and the King of Prussia
provided for the reorganization of Germany to their
own advantage.   According to this document Russia
was to advance into Poland and Prussia was to expand
into northwest Germany, into lands already earmarked
for Hanover and contemplated too as exchanges to
Denmark for Norway or as compensation to Sweden.
The Convention also provided for a Council of Ad-

---

[5] The German historians exaggerated the "Austrasian" project, as
Webster points out (*Castlereagh*, 105); Schinkel likewise overstates it
(*Minnen*, VII, 94).   On Carl Johan's relations with Stein and Münster
and their plans see T. T. Höjer, "Sverige och det tyska rekonstruktionsproblemet," *Historisk Tidskrift* (1933), 1-81; Hormayr, *Lebensbilder aus
dem Befreiungskriege: Münster* (3 vols., 1844-1845.)

[6] Schinkel, *Minnen*, VII, 84-92, and *Bihang*, III, 88-109.   According to
Schinkel Count Wangenheim even proposed that Bernadotte be king of a
united North Germany.   Herr Sieveking of Hamburg spoke of Bernadotte
as heir of both Sully and Gustavus Adolphus, and wished him to become
protector of a German confederation (Höjer, "En Hanseatisk Karl Johansbeundrare . . . 1813," *Historisk Tidskrift* (1934), 186-190.

ministration in reconquered German territory. In this organization neither Great Britain nor Sweden was mentioned or invited to participate. Carl Johan was bitter about this exclusion and still more so when the Russian Alopeus was appointed administrator in North Germany and asked the Prince to succor Hamburg; he protested to the Tsar and warned Alopeus that Germany would never be freed "if the Allies did not march in concert and recall their mutual engagements."[7] The Council never attained much importance, but Britain and Sweden each "assumed an invitation" and appointed a representative. Münster roundly denounced the exclusive Russo-Prussian program, fearing for Hanover. Bernadotte feared for his "footing on the continent" and his place in the German Diet, and he was wounded in his most sensitive spot— his *amour propre*. He had hoped to be the adored savior of Germany, now others managed things behind his back and he did not even have the respectable army so long promised.[8]

Within Bernadotte's own camp arose fears, antagonisms and breaches of discipline which seriously disturbed the Prince's spirit. Back in Stockholm the King had lapses of memory and might die at any moment; his death might be the signal for outbreaks

[7] Alopeus to Carl Johan, May 5/17, 1813 (copy), SRA, G. L. Sam.; Carl Johan to Alopeus, May 19, to Alexander May 21, BFA. Schinkel prints all of the latter to Alexander except the complaint about the Convention of Breslau! (*Minnen*, VII, 377-381). See also *Castlereagh Corr.*, VIII, 364, 374ff, 384ff.

[8] Münster's memoir, sent by Rehausen to Wetterstedt, May 14, SRA, Anglica; copy of Convention in *Castlereagh Corr.*, VIII, 369-371; Wetterstedt to G. Löwenhielm, May 24, SRA, G. L. Sam.; Höjer, "Sverige och . . . ," *Historisk Tidskrift* (1933), 1-81.

in spite of the popularity of the elected heir. Pessimistic Engeström warned against placing confidence in the Russians, and advised Carl Johan to shed no Swedish blood in the war.[9] A controversy on the war policy broke out in the press between two indiscreet editors, Grevesmöhlen and Wallmark; Carl Johan suspected a Danish plot behind Wallmark's diatribe, and took immediate action prohibiting political articles. The incident left a bitter taste in his mouth as he left Sweden for the continent, threatening alternately vengeance and retirement.[10]

The uncurbed independence of the Swedish officers expressed itself in *skåls* to Hamburg and in memoirs on how to conduct the war without Russian aid. Even Wetterstedt was discontented with the long delay and "wished only that we could . . . do something and write less."[11] The most spectacular breach of discipline was the Anckarsvärd incident. Colonel Anckarsvärd, Russophobe, ambitious, and hot-headed, first absented himself from reviews and then wrote an impassioned letter to Carl Johan referring to the bitter loss of Finland and the gloomy outlook for Norway, and concluding with a reminder to the Prince of the 1809 revolution and the possibility of another one.

[9] June 21, 1813, Engeström, *Minnen*, II, 357-359. Cf. Schück, *Skjöldebrands Memoarer*, V, 50, and Schinkel, *Minnen*, VII, 99-100. See also protocol of the Swedish council, Apr. 2, SRA, U.D. 60-11. Skåne was the center of discontent in Sweden, under the influence of the poet, Tegnér.

[10] An excellent summary is Helge Almquist's "Karl Johan, Utrikespolitiken och Pressen år 1813," *Scandia*, II (1929), 134ff.

[11] To Engeström, June 21, 1813 (also May 29), Stockholm KB, Engeström Samling. On the general state of feeling see also Rein, *Adlercreutz* (2 vols., Helsingfors, 1927); Johan Feuk, "Carl Axel Löwenhielms Lefvernesbeskrifning," *Historisk Tidskrft* (1925), 132-152; *Skjöldebrands Memoarer*, V, 25-26; Schinkel, *Minnen*, VII, esp. 398-399.

His punishment was only dismissal and a brief confinement on his father's estates, but Anckarsvärd never forgot his disgrace, and exchanged letters with General Döbeln, who had disobeyed orders at Hamburg, about *"den fördömde fransosen"* ("that damned Frenchman").[12] Bernadotte was anguished by these outbreaks of rancor and poor judgment, and since he never learned Swedish he found it difficult to establish really intimate contact with his officers and men. Perhaps his slow-moving caution in the war was due partly to smouldering suspicion of his own army.

The bevy of foreigners at Bernadotte's perambulating court was both an aid and an irritation. August W. Schlegel, the German author, had followed the Prince since mid-winter, writing propagandist tracts on German politics and the Continental System. The following winter Benjamin Constant helped in similar activities. Madame de Staël for a time exercised some influence from London (she had been in Stockholm during the winter 1812-1813), but her son Albert was killed in a duel during the armistice and her other son, placed in the Swedish Legation in London, never won the confidence of Minister Rehausen.[13]

Friendly Thornton and meek Suchtelen followed Carl Johan from Stockholm. Great Britain sent out

[12] Enander, "Carl Henrik Anckarsvärd och disciplinbrottet 1813," *Personhistorisk Tidskrift*, XXXI (1930), 174-198, is an admirable treatment. In the BFA are some letters to which Enander did not have access which portray Bernadotte's forgiving spirit (to Carl XIII, July 3, 5, 1813).

[13] Ahnfelt, II, 247-248; Schlegel to Münster, June 5, 1813 (copy), SRA, C. J. Papper 88; see also my introduction to "Benjamin Constant's *Projet Corrigé*," *Journal of Modern History*, VII (1935), 41f and below, p. 102. Madame de Staël's *Appeal to the Nations of Europe against the Continental System* was published originally in Stockholm, "by authority of Bernadotte."

also General Hope and Castlereagh's brother Sir
Charles Stewart, and the Tsar got his more critical
information through the spying Corsican, Pozzo di
Borgo.  Count Neipperg and later Count Vincent rep-
resented Austria, and General Krusemarck and General
Kalkreuth guarded Prussian interests.  The suspicions
and the advice of this group, particularly of Pozzo di
Borgo, kept Bernadotte in a constant turmoil.

With his allies Bernadotte's uncertain relations were
made even more critical by the armistice.  Great
Britain, annoyed by her purchase of aid from an ex-
marshal of France with Norwegian territory and British money, at least wanted to see the marshal fight.
Other states, too, were seeking to obtain the greatest
advantages to themselves with the least possible exertion.  Metternich admitted that Austrian coöperation depended to a large extent on Bernadotte's policy
and suggested for a plan of campaign that the Austrian
army take an *"attitude offensive, mais qu'elle restat sur
la défensive"*; that the Russians and Prussians take an
*"attitude offensive mesurée,"* but that the Prince's corps
take a *"vigoureuse offensive pour déloger Napoléon de la
gauche de l'Elbe."*[14]
Metternich likewise used his control of the military
balance of power to determine the whole question of
peace or war.  He stated the terms on which Austria
would stand for peace: (1) dissolution of the Duchy
of Warsaw, (2) enlargement of Prussia, (3) restoration
of Illyria to Austria, (4) reëstablishment of the Hanse

[14] Oncken, *Oesterreich und Preussen,* II, 673 and see 410ff; cf. Forssell
*Wetterstedt,* 191ff.

towns—at least Hamburg and Lübeck. To these essential points others were added as desirable: (5) the abolition of the Confederation of the Rhine and (6) the restoration of Prussia as of 1806. No mention of British interests, no mention of Swedish interests. These were only general bases, of course, but they showed Austria's indifference or hostility to the matters not mentioned. Such was the foundation on which Metternich signed the secret treaty of Reichenbach with Russia and Prussia, and discussed with Napoleon in the famous Dresden interview. And it was Metternich who, on his own responsibility, extended the armistice to August 10.[15]

These moves behind the scenes and the need for concerted action made Bernadotte anxious to confer with his allies and the armistice provided the opportunity. Skjöldebrand, therefore, went to the Russo-Prussian headquarters to make the arrangements, and when Alexander at length wrote Bernadotte suggesting a meeting at the castle of Trachenberg in Silesia the Crown Prince accepted immediately.[16] Bernadotte traveled a long and rough journey through the byways of northern Germany to reach Trachenberg on July 9, 1813. Perhaps wounded dignity slowed his feet, and the memory of the many slights he had received— the Dolgorouki mission, the Tsar's delays, the only

[15] Webster, *Castlereagh*, 137-141. G. Löwenhielm knew the Austrian six points, but not the distinction between the four and the two, (to Carl Johan, June 17, SRA). He was as ignorant as were the British of the treaty of Reichenbach.

[16] Skjöldebrand to Carl Johan, June 21, and "Borjan af Juli," 1813, SRA, Diverse; G. Löwenhielm to Wetterstedt, June 21, SRA; Alexander to Carl Johan, June 16/28, 18/30, SRA, Främ. Suv.; Schück, *Skjöldebrands Memoarer*, V, 12-18.

recently ratified Prussian treaty, the lack of troops—
for he arrived at the meeting place not until midnight,
and the sovereigns had waited dinner for hours.  His
advisers feared then that his frigidity would wreck
good feeling.[17]

A whole galaxy of talent was present.  Wetterstedt
and General Stedingk had come with the Prince, and
Gustav Löwenhielm came from Reichenbach.  Suchtelen was there, Stadion from Austria, and the British
envoys Cathcart and Thornton; even the Prussian
Crown Prince came the second day with Professor
Ancillon.  Generals Toll, Volkonsky, Knesebeck, and
a bevy of Russian and Prussian diplomats headed by
Nesselrode and Hardenberg filled in the background.

Through the first twenty-four hours of greetings and
miscellaneous conversations Bernadotte felt his way
warily.  The monarchs quickly convinced him they
meant to renew the war, but they found it difficult to
satisfy him on Austria's attitude.  He asked if Austria
had given any written pledge, and no one dared divulge
the sole, secret, treaty of Reichenbach.  As evidence
of Austria's firmness they cited the angry argument at
Dresden between Metternich and Napoleon, and a
letter to Alexander from the Emperor Francis promising war if Napoleon refused any of the six points.[18]

On the second day (July 11) Bernadotte spent the
whole forenoon and part of the afternoon closeted with
Count Stadion—himself an indication of Austria's de-

---

[17] G. Löwenhielm's "Svar till Schinkel," SRA, G. L. Sam.; Schinkel,
*Minnen*, VII, 181-188; Suremain, 304; Stedingk, 221f; Tingsten, 192.
Oncken (*op. cit.*, 421ff) treats the meeting very carelessly, but Woynar
(88ff) has handled him roughly for it.

[18] Wetterstedt to Engeström, July 11, 1813, SRA.

sire to please, for he was a known Napoleon-hater. Through a conversation which grew more and more friendly Stadion reassured Bernadotte by tracing the trend of Austrian policy through the past sixteen months. Bernadotte spoke vivaciously but wisely, although he often digressed into interesting but irrelevant tales of his French soldiering. The afternoon discussion bore on Norway, for which Stadion had been prepared by Alexander. The Prince talked of his going to Sweden and finally said he could not have come now to the continent as a knight-errant, but only to gain advantage for Sweden; he must acquire Norway, and he wanted to know how Austria stood on the question. Stadion explained that Austria considered the problem as belonging primarily to Britain and Scandinavia, and therefore did not mention it in her negotiations with France; if a general peace congress eventuated Sweden's interests would naturally be in the first line. If, on the other hand, the Prague negotiations were fruitless and Austria joined in the war, it appeared to him indubitable:

"Qu'alors il devait y avoir une réciprocité parfaite d'engagemens et que dès que la Suède combattait avec l'Autriche pour la même cause, la cour de Vienne aurait à accéder aux engagemens qu'avaient pris la Russie et la Prusse envers la cour de Stockholm, tout comme cette dernière devrait se joindre à ceux qui auraient peutêtre pris jusque là entre l'Autriche et les puissances coalisées."[19]

Bernadotte caught at this statement and made Stadion repeat it several times; it seemed to satisfy him com-

---

[19] Stadion to Metternich, July 14, 1813, Woynar, 160-170.

pletely. For making this unauthorized promise Stadion
had to excuse himself to Metternich: circumstances demanded it, he said, and it bound Austria to nothing
unless Sweden actually fought with and for her, in
which case the Emperor could hardly cavil at a conquest which could create no serious complications.
All in all, both Stadion and Bernadotte seemed content with the day's work.[20]

In order to clinch the Norwegian matter Wetterstedt
wrote to the Russian and Prussian Ministers asking
renewed assurances that in case of peace Russia and
Prussia promise to require Napoleon's approval of the
cession. Both politely refused on the ground that it
was best to keep Napoleon out of this purely northern
affair, and that Denmark would have to be brought
within the treaty pacification herself. The allies evidently wanted Sweden to act before being paid any
more promises, although that evening the Tsar definitely promised the Prince to break diplomatic relations with Denmark.[21] With these pledges Sweden
had to be content.

For the sake of Austrian good feeling Carl Johan
agreed with Alexander and Frederick William that it
was best to sanction the continuation of the armistice,
but he insisted that his safety and the added expense
to Sweden and Great Britain forbade any further delay. He rejected the indirect invitation to participate
in the Prague conference on the grounds that Norway

[20] *Ibid.*; also Wetterstedt to Engeström, July 11, SRA.

[21] Wetterstedt to Rehausen, July 11, 17, 1813, enclosing various copies
SRA, Anglica; Stadion to Metternich, July 14, Woynar, 169; Alexander to
Carl Johan, July 24, SRA, Främ. Suv.

was not on the agenda, and that the London government might misunderstand.[22]   He was inclined to be
both magnanimous and hopeful, for by evening of the
eleventh of July he had succeeded in his most immediate
aim: he had the promise of 22,000 Russians (the corps
of Winzingerode, Woronzov, Tettenborn, and Czernis-
cheff) and 40,000 Prussians (all of Bülow's force, part
of Tauenzien's, and some landwehr battalions).   With
Wallmoden's 10,000 (German Legion, Hanseats, and
Mecklenburgers) and his 30,000 Swedes he had 100,000
men, an army which both satisfied his dignity and enabled him to act decisively.

On July 12, the third day of the conference, the
news of Wellington's triumph at Vitoria invigorated
the meeting with increasing hope, and made Austrian
accession more probable.   Bernadotte himself was personally pleased to receive by courier a flattering note
from the Emperor Francis; it promised nothing, but
implied Austrian coöperation, hence Bernadotte and
Stadion expressed anew the mutual regard and need
of Austria and Sweden.[23]

The military discussions did not crystallize into the
"Trachenberg Plan" until afternoon of the twelfth.
Patriotic Prussians cannot admit that Bernadotte developed the plan by which Napoleon was defeated,
and have inaugurated a debate which will perhaps be
endless.   The suggestion that there was no plan is
ridiculous, and the claims for Toll's or Knesebeck's

[22] Fain, *Manuscrit de mil huit cent treize* . . . (2 vols., Paris, 1824), II,
155-157; Wetterstedt to Rehausen, July 11, SRA, Anglica; Thornton to
Castlereagh, July 12, London FO, Sweden 82.

[23] Schinkel, *Minnen*, VII, 408-409 and 191; G. Löwenhielm's "Svar till
Schinkel-Tillägg," SRA, G. L. Sam.

authorship are based almost solely on national pride. Radetzky, the Austrian, may deserve some consideration, for on July 7 he drew up a plan similar to the Trachenberg agreement; but he sent this to Schwarzenberg and the Emperor, and it could hardly have influenced discussions before July 20. Its general ideas might have reached Bernadotte through Stadion, but Stadion was not a military man; he merely mentioned in a despatch that the Prince approved of some military suggestions he made—he did not say what these were, and probably they were Metternich's suggestions of June; and the protocol of Trachenberg was written after Stadion left. Suffice it then to say that Bernadotte assumed credit for the plan, it was perfectly consistent with his methods, the Tsar and General Schwarzenberg and Cathcart explicitly recognized his authorship, and it was the Swedish general, Count Gustav Löwenhielm, who wrote out the protocol on the orders of Bernadotte.[24]

Before the plan was adumbrated Bernadotte had announced the principles on which it should be based: Assuming Austrian coöperation there should be three main armies: (1) the Bohemian, the largest, composed of Russian and Austrian forces; (2) the Silesian, of Prussian soldiers under Blücher; and (3) the Army of North Germany, a mixed force under the Crown Prince of Sweden. These forces should converge on Napoleon in a great semi-circle, attacking detached corps, but giving way before large numbers; if Napoleon in person concentrated against any one of the armies it was

[24] See especially Sam Clason, in a lecture and bibliographical critique in *Karl Johan Förbundets Handlingar . . . 1911-1914*, 41-87.

to withdraw while the others closed in on Napoleon's flanks and attacked his communications. In dealing with a warrior genius one must wear away his strength bit by bit, not allow him to deal a decisive blow. Special detachments should harass the French, utilizing the friendliness of the territory; others should guard the French forts on the Elbe and the Oder. Napoleon's area should be diminished until at length he should be forced to meet all three armies at once, and then the Bohemian army should destroy him. If he did not allow the belt to contract about him he should be forced to run from one army to another, losing land, time, and men. Light troops should harass him night and day. Each of the allied armies should have a confidential officer in the camps of the others to promote unity. Supplies and reserves should be carefully provided. In order that the enemy's central position be not used to destroy the allies in detail each should begin operations at once. Briefly, the plan called for a great semi-circular wall of men, flexible at the point of massed attack, but steadily contracting about Napoleon, strangling his army.[25]

The protocol applied these principles. The main forces, it prescribed, should take a stand in the "salient bastion" of the Bohemian mountains, and should be increased to about 220,000 by the transfer of 100,000 from the then large Silesian army. The Crown Prince should leave 15,000-20,000 to guard Denmark and the Hanse towns, and with 70,000-80,000 concentrate on Treuenbreitzein; when the armistice ended he should force a crossing of the Elbe between Torgau and

Magdeburg and advance toward Leipzig. Blücher's Army of Silesia, left with 50,000-80,000 should avoid battle unless sure of victory and push toward the Elbe and Carl Johan, ready also if necessary to reinforce the Army of Bohemia. The main body should debouch as circumstances indicated at Eger and Hof, in Silesia, in Saxony, or along the Danube. If Napoleon attacked either the Bohemian or the North German army the other was to advance vigorously on his rear. "All the allied armies will take the offensive and the camp of the enemy will be their rendezvous." Bennigsen's reserve should come up to Glogau and the militia should watch the forts on the Elbe and the Oder.[26]

As soon as the protocol was written the conference broke up—Monday afternoon, July 12, 1813. In a pouring rain the Russians and Prussians returned to Reichenbach and the Swedes started the three-day journey to Stralsund. Troops of Cossacks guarded their carriages as they rumbled northward pondering the new aspect of affairs. The Prague negotiations

[26] d'Angeberg [Chodzko], *Le Congrès de Vienne et les Traités de 1815* (2 vols., Paris, 1864), I, 25-26; Bernhardi, *Denkwurdigkeiten aus dem Leben . . . Grafen von Toll* (4 vols. in 5, Leipzig, 1865-1866), III, 80-82; Schinkel, *Minnen*, VII, 200-202.

What seems a plausible hypothesis in the dispute as to the authorship of the protocol, is that Carl Johan stated the general principles and that General Toll made the specific application. There are, however, many absolute contradictions in the evidence. One peculiar thing is that Toll did not sign the protocol—it was signed only by Gustav Löwenhielm, Knesebeck, and Volkonsky. It should be remarked that in June, Carl Johan had proposed three campaign plans. One involved an attack on Holstein; the others a masking of Denmark and Hamburg allowing action either independently from Berlin, or in coöperation with the main army in central Germany. (Clason, *op. cit.*, 76-79; Schück, *Skjöldebrands Memoarer*, V, 15-16).

they knew were unlikely to bring peace, and Austria was almost certain to join in the war. Carl Johan had not been asked to be commander-in-chief, but he had obtained a large army and proof of his allies' good faith. He had been persuaded that Austria was not as intransigent on Norway as he had feared. His plan of attacking Denmark first had already been rejected, and he had set himself to perfect a plan of direct operations in consonance with the general desire.[27] The hopes of the coalition on July 12 were brighter than they had ever been before.

The peace negotiations in Prague sputtered fitfully due to Napoleon's inept procrastination and the swelling war sentiment among the allies. Austria was doubtless glad that Sweden refused the half-hearted invitations to join, and Austria along with the others planned zealously for war. Then at the eleventh hour Great Britain accepted Austria's mediation. When this news reached Stralsund, August 5, Carl Johan was away, and Wetterstedt was so upset that he wrote Löwenhielm that although Sweden would follow Britain's lead she must insist that the armistice be denounced August 10; otherwise subsidies would probably cease and soon the bad season would set in; hence Löwenhielm should declare that *"si l'armistice est prolongée, [la Suède] Se verra forcée d'abandonne le Continent."*[28]

The next day Bernadotte returned and was startled

[27] Despite later events I think Oncken is absolutely unjustified in the accusation that Carl Johan planned in advance a campaign in which his Swedish troops would take no active part (Oncken, *op. cit.*, II, 421ff).

[28] Wetterstedt to Löwenhielm, Aug. 5, 1813, SRA.

by the hasty words of the usually steady chancellor. Within an hour Wetterstedt was writing a new despatch cancelling all threats.[29]  The Prince might have his passionate outbursts, but they were verbal gasconades from which he could extricate himself a few hours later; not yet would he officially threaten withdrawal on a contingency of slight significance, and thus give his allies the chance to call him deserter.  Bernadotte remembered that his gains depended on his teammates, and that he needed British aid for an attack on Zealand. The outlook was too hopeful to make him wish to create any ill-feeling.  In any case the late British concessions did not retard the progress of events.  On August 10 the long period of waiting and delay ended. War began.

[29] Wetterstedt to Löwenhielm, Aug. 6, 1813, SRA.

# V

## The Leipzig Campaign

### *August to October 1813*

In the early hours of August 11, 1813, the allies formally denounced the armistice. On August 12 Austria declared war on France. On August 17 the new campaign opened. Within the next eight months the power of Napoleon was to be obliterated in Germany, Italy, Holland, and France, and the master of Europe was to become Emperor of the Island of Elba.

For Bernadotte and his Army of the North the campaign opened brilliantly. On August 23 he met Oudinot leading part of a converging French attack on Berlin. On the flat plain of Grossbeeren Bernadotte skilfully disposed his troops so that the enthusiastic Prussian soldiery under Bülow repelled Oudinot's men. The French left wing had marched more slowly, and retreated when they heard of Oudinot's defeat, therefore the Russian and Swedish forces in reserve did not engage in battle. Thus was checked the first French attempt to regain north Germany and reëstablish contact with the garrisons on the Oder.[1]

---

[1] The treatment of the military maneuvers which follows is based mainly on these well-known works: Friederich, *Der Herbstfeldzuges 1813* (3 vols., Berlin, 1903-1906), the most exhaustive study of the campaign; Quistorp, *Geschichte der Nord-Armee im Jahre 1813* (Berlin, 1859); Maude, *The Leipzig*

In the center the French retreated before Blücher, then Blücher retreated when the long shouts of the French announced Napoleon's arrival. But the Emperor did not remain, and on August 26 Blücher turned on his pursuers and mercilessly chastised them at the Katzbach. The Grand Army of Bohemia had deflected its course to capture Dresden. Just before the moment of attack wild cheers told the allies that Napoleon had come, and they shrank from action. But their signal was fired by mistake. Soon Napoleon, utilizing the numbers which his short interior lines had enabled him to throw into the city, plunged the allies into retreat over the rain-soaked roads to Bohemia. Only a combination of luck and heroic fighting saved the retreat from becoming a rout, and led to the overwhelming of Vandamme's pursuit corps (at Kulm, August 30).

The Trachenberg Plan was being followed in spirit and in letter. Bernadotte pushed on southward from Grossbeeren, facing Oudinot's outposts at Wittenberg. But he knew that the repulse at Grossbeeren would bring a renewed drive by the French. His numerous spies informed him of Napoleon's plan to send 120,000

---

*Campaign 1813* (London, 1908), which has good maps and is based on Friederich; Tingsten, *Huvuddragen av Sveriges Krig och Yttre Politik augusti 1813-januari 1814* (Stockholm, 1924), the second in General Tingsten's three volume study, careful, up-to-date; Wiehr, *Napoleon und Bernadotte im Herbstfeldzuge 1813* (Berlin, 1883); and the *Recueil des Ordres de Mouvement*, etc. Specific references to these books are given only when doubt or contradiction necessitates them.

A new study by Konrad Lehmann, *Die Rettung Berlins im Jahre 1813* (Berlin, 1934), highly praises Bernadotte's strategy and belittles the work of the Prussians; Lehmann also argues that Oudinot was not driving toward Berlin, but trying to break through the allied lines to make a flank attack on Blücher in conjunction with Macdonald.

men through to Berlin, so Bernadotte pled for reinforcements, and got 10,000 Prussians from Bennigsen's
army. Moreau had already said the position of the
Crown Prince's army was too hazardous, but Bernadotte wanted to act in the north in order to maintain
contact with Sweden, and also because he held an exaggerated idea of the importance of Berlin.[2]

When Napoleon had gathered in the information of
Grossbeeren, the Katzbach, Kulm, and the check of
Davoust in Mecklenburg, he gave up his scheme of
marching on Prague, and sent Ney to supersede Oudinot
and prepare for a powerful main offensive through
Berlin. Blücher, however, was continuing to press
Macdonald's army so roughly that Napoleon had to
go to Macdonald instead of to Ney—for which Bernadotte should have been thankful. The Emperor was
now anxious to overwhelm the ex-marshal whom he
had once said *"ne fera que piaffer."* After Grossbeeren
he wrote to Ney, *"Gardez-vous de Bernadotte, car il est
fin. Pour les autres canailles, je m'en fous."*[3]

On the third of September Ney reached Wittenberg,
on the fifth he was marching to Baruth to collect more
men and proceed for Berlin. After a bloody skirmish
with Tauenzien he reached Dennewitz. But dust
clouds warned Bernadotte of the French advance, and
he maneuvered his entire army for battle. The next
morning Tauenzien's little force was just beginning to

---

[2] Tingsten, *Huvuddragen . . . 1813-1814,* 28-30; Wetterstedt to Rehausen, Aug. 17, 1813, SRA, Anglica. The Prussians did not consider
Berlin as important as did Carl Johan; there is even a story that the Prussian
generals likened their capital to a loose woman already so frequently violated that she had no claim to protection (Schinkel, *Minnen,* VII, 194).

[3] Tingsten, *Huvuddragen . . . 1813-1814,* 26.

falter when Bülow reached the field. His rabid Prussians put up a terrific struggle, and the Swedish and Russian artillery completed the disintegration of Ney's command: the second French thrust to the North was parried.

The battle of guns was soon over; the battle of words it engendered still booms. No one disputes that the troops were cleverly disposed and the victory thorough, although the pursuit was inefficient. But the Prussians lost 10,000 men, the Swedes none, and only twelve wounded. At Dennewitz as at Grossbeeren Bülow's corps did the lion's share of the fighting and the Swedes were held in reserve. Pozzo di Borgo and the Austrian General Vincent bitterly charged that Bernadotte could have thrown 40,000 more into battle and exterminated the French, that his orders were slow and uncertain, that he was out of reach for an hour [eluding Pozzo?] and that he criticised Bülow's operations openly.[4] The Swedes themselves were angry, and at a banquet in Coswig General Skjöldebrand told the Prince how humiliated he had been at the order to halt his cavalry just as they were to come upon the enemy. In reply Bernadotte laid bare his idea:

"You wish, then, that I should let the Swedish army take part in every encounter, and so dissolve itself through losses that I have no army of my own left? And how shall one know that the whole strength will not be needed for Sweden's own affair, when the problem is to take Norway?"[5]

[4] Pozzo to Nesselrode, Aug. 26/Sept. 7, 1813 (secret), Upsala, Alin Samling XII; Vincent to Metternich, Sept. 7, Vienna SA; *Castlereagh Corr.*, IX, 48-51, 52-59. Cf. Lehmann, *op. cit.*, ch. v, vi.

[5] Schück, *Skjöldebrands Memoarer*, V, 51. On Carl Johan's clever manipulations of troops, *ibid.*, 42ff; Suremain, 312f.

This obvious sparing of the Swedes brought on Bernadotte the condemnation of Thornton, Pozzo, all the Prussians, even his own Swedes, and in distant England a sportsmanlike nation looked askance. It is not to be wondered at that Bernadotte did not share the Prussians' lust for extermination of all Frenchmen. Also, the cause was Prussia's and the continent's much more than it was Sweden's. Yet Bernadotte had agreed to play the game, and the calculating way he played it cast a shadow over the glory of his victories.

After Dennewitz the campaign seemed to settle into a war of attrition. The allies had blocked Napoleon in every direction, but could not press home their advantages. Bernadotte dared not advance with his small force. Even Blücher despite his zeal had to restrain himself, though he insisted on remaining independent. Only the huge army in Bohemia was capable of aggressive action, and after its defeat at Dresden it lay frightened and impotent. Löwenhielm urged action there to save the Army of the North from destruction, but these 250,000 remained almost stationary until the end of September.

The hot-headed Prussians and the military-political agents urged Bernadotte to press boldly forward, but he kept his eye on the torpor in Bohemia and insisted on possessing the French posts before he advanced.

In 1814, when the Norway campaign did materialize, Carl Johan admitted his policy of safeguarding the Swedes, telling the Prussians that if they would send him a detachment he would use it in Sweden's cause with as much caution as he had formerly used the Swedes in what was essentially Prussia's cause. (Tarrach to Frederick William III, June 7, 1814, Berlin SA, Corr.).

Napoleon's northward threat against Grossenhain vin-
dicated Bernadotte's judgment and for a time silenced
his importunate advisers.  Disputes began again when
the Prince ordered Bülow, who itched for action, to
take the important fortification at Wittenberg.  The
task was beyond Bülow's means and filled to overflowing his cup of resentment; he remonstrated in
offensive terms and Bernadotte dashed off a demand
to Frederick William to reprimand his general for
breach of discipline.  Such intractability from a Prussian officer was intolerable to a former Marshal of
France and Minister of War.  Late in September
Gneisenau, the brains of Blücher's army, actually proposed that Tauenzien and Bülow transfer to Blücher's
command, because Gneisenau mistrusted Bernadotte's
"weak character" and his Swedish interests.  For
Bülow this transfer would have been violation of contract, but Tauenzien's corps was only "attached."
Hence the Crown Prince demanded that Tauenzien
be put strictly under his orders.[6]

The general lack of confidence threatened sad results.  The supposedly friendly Tsar, for example, had
replaced kindly old Suchtelen with the acrimonious
Pozzo di Borgo, and had instructed him to see that
the Prince's personal considerations did not interfere
with his action for the common cause.[7]  Since the all-
night session at Carlscrona Pozzo's suspicions of Bernadotte were as strong as his hate of Napoleon.  Perhaps

---

[6] Wetterstedt to Löwenhielm, Oct. 2, 1813, SRA; *Castlereagh Corr.*, IX,
58-59.  Frederick William specifically ordered Bülow to obey Carl Johan
(Schinkel, *Minnen*, VII, 412-413).  See also, *Recueil*, 174-175.

[7] Instructions for Pozzo, July 31/Aug. 12, 1813, Upsala, Alin Samling.

in each case his feelings were tinged with a sense of the injustice of that fate which raised two other commoners to thrones and overlooked the genius of Pozzo di Borgo. His instructions made him guard and adviser, his disposition made him spy and critic. Quite naturally the Prussian Krusemarck and the Austrian Vincent, who arrived at Bernadotte's headquarters late in August, were influenced by the clever Corsican. Thornton and Stewart were more independent and less prying.

According to the reports of the keen and critical Corsican the Gascon was changeable as a chameleon, illimitably ambitious, suspicious, more arrogant than Napoleon, unconstrained in passionate outbursts of temper; he was a talented strategist on a small scale, but indecision and distrust made him better able to carry out the plans of another than to formulate his own; he tried to play too many rôles to succeed in any one. Pozzo described Bernadotte's desire to pose as liberator of the French, and his feeling of brotherhood with the soldiers against whom he fought; he said the Prince had no sinister views, yet could not reconcile his personal ambitions with the work the coalition wanted done.[8] Pozzo charged specifically that Bernadotte spared the French whenever possible. Certainly he was a prudent warrior, and his character was repugnant to the pursuit and slaughter relished by the Prussians. Yet he ordered a pursuit after Dennewitz, and the order failed to reach the Swedish

---

[8] Pozzo to Nesselrode, Aug. 28/Sept. 9, et seq., Upsala, Alin Samling XII; see also Castlereagh Corr., IX, 48-51; Raabe, "Pozzo di Borgo om Karl Johan och Hans Planer, 1813," Lunds Dagblad, Jan. 2, 1924.

cavalry only because of dislocation of forces in the darkness; next day some 13,000-14,000 prisoners were picked up.[9] That he personally interested himself in French prisoners is perfectly clear—probably from mixed motives of policy and humanity.

After Dennewitz he showed this combined policy and sentiment when he learned that Colonel Clouet, an aide-de-camp of Ney, had been wounded and captured. The Prince offered him money and even parole, and then used the capture as an excuse to write Ney pleading for peace, ending with this appeal:

"Depuis long-temps nous ravageons la terre, et nous n'avons encore rien fait pour l'humanité. La confiance dont vous jouissez à si juste titre auprès de l'empereur Napoléon pourrait, ce me semble, être de quelque poids pour déterminer ce souverain à accepter enfin la paix honorable et générale qu'on lui a offerte et qu'il a repoussée. Cette gloire, prince, est digne d'un guerrier tel que vous, et le peuple francais rangerait cet éminent service au nombre de ceux que nous lui rendions, il y a vingt ans, sous les murs de Saint-Quentin, en combattant pour sa liberté et pour son indépendance."[10]

Bernadotte showed the letter to the diplomatic representatives but they, with their prosaic conceptions that war could be waged only with powder and shell, unanimously disapproved; they were doubly afraid of any such attempt at an undermining propaganda by an ex-Frenchman. Bernadotte in turn was disgusted at the allies' blindness to the use of "moral forces" and continued to try to create distrust between Napoleon and his marshals by such means as inordinate

[9] Above cited reports; also Tingsten, *Huvuddragen . . . 1813-1814*, 112-143; Schück, *Skjöldebrands Memoarer*, V, 47-50.
[10] Sept. 9, 1813, Sarrans, *Histoire de Bernadotte . . .* , II, 361.

praise of the Prince of Neufchatel in a bulletin.[11] Such methods made people suspicious, but they were too open to be treacherous. Probably Bernadotte hoped thus to create a party in his favor in the French army, but this in itself was harmless to the allies, and behind any personal ambitions is evident a keen knowledge of psychology. Bernadotte, guided and aided by Madame de Staël, August Schlegel, and Benjamin Constant, gives us the only example outside France in this period of the deliberate use of propaganda for demoralizing the enemy. He used these methods more consciously and more thoroughly than did Napoleon, and thus furnished a foretaste of World War tactics.

Bernadotte was in fact ready to use any means he could think of to accomplish his objects. He tried, for instance, to bribe the surrender of Cüstrin and Stettin. To aid in the "persuasion" at Stettin he sent Tauenzien a letter for general consumption telling of the great forces he was going to send against the city: militia, reserves, 2000 English, and a flotilla under Admiral Cederström. Then he sent Tauenzien a private letter saying that all these threats were false, but that he wished offers made.[12] He did not have the 100,000 riksdalers he mentioned but probably expected to get money from London.

In attempts to raise new German levies, Carl Johan announced the formation of a new "Legion" of volunteers, prisoners and deserters from the French; the

[11] *Castlereagh Corr.*, IX, 51-52, 54, 56; Löwenhielm to Carl Johan, Sept. 24, to Wetterstedt, Sept. 24 (private Ap.), Wetterstedt to Löwen, hielm, Sept. 30, SRA. Cf. Sarrans, II, 51-52.

[12] To Tauenzien, Sept. 13, 1813, BFA. A garbled pretense at a copy is printed in *Recueil*, 238. The "ostensible" letter I have not found.

Legion would operate only up to the Rhine (a provision which made Pozzo suspect wicked designs). This proclamation, disseminated widely in the French ranks, brought a *bloc* desertion from Napoleon of about 300 Saxons on September 23, and probably influenced the larger desertion during the battle of Leipzig. The Prince was especially popular with the Saxons, whom he had commanded at Wagram. Ney now wrote Napoleon that the Saxon troops were in a hopeless state. Officers openly toasted Carl Johan, and the King of Saxony had to issue a proclamation begging the soldiers not to go over to the allies. Napoleon ordered an officer to "arrest, judge, and shoot" the merchant who had taken the Swedish appeal to Frankfort.[13] When the Prince saw the demoralizing effect of this move he proposed also a Holland Legion to be headed by Suchtelen, a former Hollander, but the British disapproved this.[14] Bernadotte, son of the Revolution, realized to the full that the War of Liberation was a great national rising, and he was ready to take advantage of all this implied; he would raise the masses, he would arm enthusiasm.

While being held inactive by the inactivity of the Army of Bohemia, Bernadotte cast anxious eyes be-

---

[13] Wetterstedt to Löwenhielm, Sept. 8, 25, 1813, SRA; Order of the Day, Sept. 11 (copy in Wetterstedt to Rehausen Sept. 11), SRA, Anglica; "Proclamation Le Prince Royal de Suède aux Saxons," *Recueil*, 227-228; Pozzo to Nesselrode, Sept. 2/14, Upsala, Alin Samling XII; Carl Johan to Alexander, Frederick William, and Francis, Sept. 14, BFA; Fain, *1813*, II, 357-358; Ney to Napoleon, Sept. 23-24 (extract), Sarrans, II, 54-55 note; Napoleon to Neufchatel, Sept. 24, Lecestre, *Lettres*, II, 289.

[14] Carl Johan to Suchtelen, Oct. 6, 1813, BFA; Renier, *Great Britain and the Establishment of the Netherlands 1813-1815*. See also below on the military memorandum of Sept. 24, pp. 104ff.

hind him on Denmark. On September 19 he ordered
General Vegesack to attack the Danes if Davoust withdrew his support, and on September 30 he ordered
Wallmoden to attack Davoust.[15] He knew that if he
were defeated the Danes would invade southern
Sweden, and he feared also a Russian reconciliation
with Denmark. One day when he despondently feared
a plot to remove Wallmoden's corps from the Danish
border, Vincent and prying Pozzo entered and asked
for news of Wallmoden. Gascon blood heated up in
a fifteen minute lecture; then Pozzo exploded the dyna-
mite by asking if Bernadotte intended to use the
Prussians against Denmark. Bernadotte burst forth
in fury: he led his army where he pleased, he had
been elevated by his own deeds, he owed nothing to
sovereigns, everything to the masses. He cited the
Prussians their history and claimed generosity because
he did not capture Frederick William after the battle
of Jena. As he became fatigued his arrogance sub-
sided, and he tried to cajole all into parting as friends.
Next day he was ill. Such, said Pozzo, was the man
with whom delicate problems had to be discussed, and
added, *"rien n'est moins sur, que ce qu'il cherche à
faire croire."* At least any side campaign against Denmark had been thwarted for the moment, and Pozzo
claimed the credit.[16]

Besides Denmark, Bernadotte was worried about
many other things. King Carl XIII was again reported

[15] Schinkel, *Minnen, Bihang,* III, 189-194; Wetterstedt to Löwenhielm,
Sept. 30, 1813, SRA.

[16] *Castlereagh Corr.,* IX, 57-59; Vincent to Metternich, Sept. 24, Vienna
SA; Pozzo to Nesselrode, Sept. 13/25 (two despatches), Sept. 15/27, Oct. 5,
Upsala, Alin Samling XII.

failing, but despite possible difficulties the Crown Prince insisted he would not leave the army. Insubordination among the Prussians, and Archduke Charles' intrigues among the Austrians both raised anxious thoughts. The British subsidies ceased in October, and no new agreement had been reached. Worst of all, if Blücher obeyed the sovereigns' desire and moved south, the Army of the North would be strategically abandoned.

However real his anxieties, and however rash his words, Bernadotte's path of action remained cautious and consistent. Blücher was eager for a joint offensive with Bernadotte, but was too proud and too suspicious to place his army under the Prince's superior command. Hence Bernadotte merely proceeded carefully to construct bridges across the Elbe and send over advanced corps. The Swedes received their baptism of fire in such a move at Dessau, September 28. While Blücher was in the rear and the main army quiescent Bernadotte could hardly be expected to push boldly forward; such a move would have left Napoleon a clear path from Dresden to Berlin and might have enabled him to separate and destroy each of the three allied armies.[17]

As a reply to criticism and as a guide for future action Bernadotte drew up a new military memorandum, dated September 24, which clearly reveals his mind at the time. He opened with a characteristic reproach against the others for their inaction. If the allies would not act together, said the Prince, they

[17] Alexander constantly urged Bernadotte to press forward, regardless of the general situation or the immobility of his own forces (to Carl Johan, Aug. 26/Sept. 7, et seq., SRA, Främ. Suv., some in Schinkel, *Bihang*, III, 179-180, *Minnen*, VII, 413-415).

should act separately, and then detailed what the Army
of the North had accomplished. The position of his
army was described: a front of one hundred leagues,
with two fortified cities (Hamburg and Lübeck), an
army and an enemy country on its right, the Elbe and
three forts in front, Grossenhain and an enemy army
on the left and Cüstrin and Stettin in the rear. Napoleon held the chord of the arc made by the allies
and was strong against Blücher and the Army of the
North. Recommendations were that Wittenberg and
Torgau should be attacked—orders had been given;
bridges and fortifications should be built on the Elbe—
it was being done; Blücher should mask Dresden, and
he and the Crown Prince should support an offensive
in Saxony by the Bohemian Army, which should rouse
the population as far as Frankfort. The allies must
use revolutionary means to combat the revolutionary
methods of Napoleon; ordinary means would be in-
adequate; *"ces moyens moraux sagement conduits"*
would produce *"un effet magique."* Once in possession
of Wittenberg and Torgau the Army of the North
would leave 30,000 men on the Elbe and march to
Leipzig or Magdeburg; the latter would be better because with it Westphalia and Hamburg would fall,
Denmark would submit, and Holland and Belgium
join the allies.[18]

Before this document reached Blücher and the sovereigns, they had all begun to do much that it advised.
While Bernadotte crept forward Blücher swung right
to join him and cross the Elbe, and the Bohemian

[18] Copies enclosed with Vincent to Metternich, Sept. 24, 1813, Vienna
SA; Wetterstedt to Engeström, Sept. 26, SRA.

Army moved to the left. The Trachenberg Plan was still operating, Napoleon was being squeezed tighter and tighter and early in October had to abandon Dresden. Bernadotte and Blücher could now support each other, so the three fronts were reduced to two and the allies outnumbered the French on each.

In the diplomatic problems which went hand in hand with the progress of the armies the allies had a disconcerting habit of making decisions without reference to the crusading Prince from the north, and the Prince had to be on the *qui vive*. German affairs were chaotic. The Austrian Emperor declined responsibility for reconstruction of the old Empire, Stein's ideas of a dual division were anathema to the Hanoverians and distasteful to the Austrians, and Metternich's idea of a network of alliances pleased no one. Bernadotte was interested in Pomerania and in Hanover, and was alert to the whole complex. When he was informed early in September that the Council of Administration had begun to function, he protested at once that no official notice had been sent the Swedes. Two weeks later Löwenhielm was told that the Council was to administer acquired territory and to distribute its income among the allies. Carl Johan "accepted," saying he assumed Sweden and Hanover would share proportionately with the others, and named Löwenhielm as the Swedish representative.[19]

Denmark lay much more heavily on Bernadotte's

[19] Wetterstedt to Vincent, Sept. 11, 1813, Vienna SA; copies of all notes sent to Rehausen, Sept. 11, SRA, Anglica; Wetterstedt to Löwenhielm, Sept. 14 *et seq.* SRA; Wetterstedt to Adlerberg, Oct. 7, SRA, Högkvarterets Koncepter.

heart than did Germany.  Thwarted repeatedly in his
plans, the ghost of the Dolgorouki mission still made
him shudder.  Now Denmark was a real threat on his
right flank.  He had pledges from Russia, Great Britain
and Prussia, but Stadion's statement at Trachenberg
proved valueless: Austria still deferred signing a treaty
with Sweden.[20]  The obvious distaste for the Swedish
program among the allies, Austria and Prussia particularly, had undoubtedly stiffened Danish resistance.
The main problem was how to bring Austria into the
group of Swedish supporters.  Very likely Bernadotte's
talk of a September offensive against Denmark was
meant to frighten the allies and Austria so that Austria
might urge Denmark to yield Norway peacefully.[21]
Bernadotte wrote to Frederick William arguing the
value of winning Denmark at once by negotiation or
by force.[22]  The alarmed King replied posthaste that
Bernadotte need not fear either Davoust or the Danes,
that the way to win Norway was by defeating Napoleon; he added that Austria had promised to take steps
in Copenhagen and that Metternich was to confer with
the Danish Minister Count Bernstorff; the best results
could be expected, so avoid an attack.[23]  Both Frederick William and Alexander had carried the Swedish
threat to Metternich and Emperor Francis, exactly as
Bernadotte must have foreseen.

The Crown Prince bombarded the Austrian officials

[20] As late as Sept. 25 Hudelist was assuring Bernstorff that Metternich
would find German compensation for Sweden, and spare Norway for Denmark (Bernstorff to Rosenkrantz, Sept. 25, DRA, Bernstorff).

[21] Vincent to Metternich, Sept. 28, 29, 1813, Vienna SA.

[22] Sept. 26, 1813, Schinkel, *Minnen, Bihang*, III, 192-194.

[23] Oct. 2, 1813, *ibid.*, III, 197-199.

directly, also. When Baron Hardegg brought him the Order of Maria Theresa he asked for a few Austrian troops for moral effect, and gave the Baron a *note verbale* on Denmark's stubbornness and her unfortunate hopes in Austria. Bernadotte and Wetterstedt deluged Vincent with arguments, especially after they had intercepted a copy of the new Danish-French treaty of July 10 and a letter from the Queen of Denmark in which the faith of Denmark in Austrian protection was openly avowed.[24] Löwenhielm pressed for the recall of the Austrian minister in Copenhagen, and got Hardenberg and Nesselrode to speak to Metternich, and the Tsar to talk with Emperor Francis. The Tsar assured Löwenhielm that Metternich had taken a peremptory tone with Bernstorff, and that now Denmark would have to yield; his own pledges were sacred and inviolable; he asked in return only that Bernadotte should not use against Holstein the forces essential for conquering Napoleon.[25]

It appeared that Carl Johan's indirect threat was about to succeed. Now he worried for fear Austria might compromise the Swedish claim. He was willing to offer the terms of May, but no more; that is, Trondhjem to Sweden at once, the rest of Norway at the peace, with a Danish option on retaining southern Norway or taking German territorial compensation. Bernadotte even considered writing to Rosenkrantz to

[24] Vincent to Metternich, Sept. 14, 19, 28, 29, 1813, Vienna SA; "Notes Remises au General Hardegg," Sept. 20, SRA, Högkv. Kon.

[25] Löwenhielm to Carl Johan, Sept. 22, Oct. 11, to Wetterstedt, Sept. 29, 30, Oct. 3, SRA; Nesselrode to Pozzo, Sept. 18/30 (copy), Vienna SA; Webster, *Castlereagh*, 158.

obviate any misunderstanding, but Vincent's protests halted this tactless though justifiable move.[26]

His worry was well-founded, but he did not visualize Metternich's methods. Metternich warned Bernstorff that Austria might have to break off relations unless, as he hoped, Denmark could improve her connections with the allies; he would await a Danish response.[27] But although this conversation was held October 1 or 2, Bernstorff did not report it until October 12 or 13, and his report did not reach Copenhagen until November 27, then being carried by the Austrian Count Bombelles. Communications were poor, but other despatches were going through. It looks like collusion between Metternich and Bernstorff: Metternich could say he had warned Denmark, yet could know that Copenhagen would not get the warning, and he had promised to await a reply. This explanation is somewhat corroborated by Metternich's letters to Vincent. One contained vague promises to show Bernadotte. Two other private notes said it was unwise to give Bernadotte details, and that the *démarche* Austria was asked to make violated her policy and could be excused only as a means of keeping the Swedes active; and Vincent was to concert everything with Pozzo, which in itself insured opposition to Sweden's policy.[28] Just so might Machiavelli have helped his enemies!

[26] Pozzo to Nesselrode, Sept. 20/Oct. 2, 1813, Upsala, Alin Samling XII; Carl Johan to Essen, Oct. 5, BFA; Wetterstedt to Bildt, Oct. 5, 8, SRA, Högkv. Kon.; Vincent to Metternich, Oct. 2, 9, Vienna SA.

[27] *Meddelelser*, VII, 397-409 (with Rosenkrantz' remarks).

[28] Metternich to Vincent, Oct. 2, 1813, Vienna SA; Wetterstedt to Engeström, Oct. 8, Bildt to Wetterstedt, Oct. 12, SRA; Friis, *Nye Aktstykker* . . . (Copenhagen, 1898), 11; cf. *Meddelelser*, VII, 392.

Taube thought a Herr Coopmans carried despatches from Bernstorff,

Nevertheless, despite the hollowness of the Austrian promises the outlook seemed hopeful for Sweden as the armies converged on Leipzig for the great trial of strength.

Contemporary opinion at Bernadotte's headquarters was that he did not wish to cross the Elbe. Letters and orders, on the other hand, indicate that he merely wanted to control Wittenberg and leave forces enough to prevent Napoleon from an attack on Berlin behind his back, then cross the Elbe and march on Leipzig. As Blücher approached, the Prince did actually move his troops over on October fourth and fifth; Blücher had crossed on October third about twenty miles upstream. Ney was forced to retire to Leipzig. Blücher insisted on following him and Carl Johan yielded, though he feared a *"coup de désespoir"* by Napoleon on the left and advocated a march straight west to the Saale.[29]

On October eighth Blücher learned that Napoleon

but he seems to have had only an impossible proposal made by von Eyben (*Meddelelser*, VII, 386-387). Another attempt at Swedish-Danish reconciliation was made through Herr von Brienen, secretary of the Russian Minister to Denmark, Lisakewitz. Von Brienen received Carl Johan's offer when passing through Swedish headquarters (Sept. 17), and took it to Lisakewitz, then residing in Malmö, Sweden. Lisakewitz hastened it on to Rosenkrantz, who interpreted it to mean that Carl Johan was becoming desperate (Oct. 6, 1813, DRA, Forestillinger; *Meddelelser*, VII, 379-382). Early in August the Hereditary Prince of Mecklenburg-Schwerin wrote to Frederick VI with Bernadotte's sanction to persuade the King to make a settlement; he wanted of course to avoid the use of Mecklenburg as compensation for Norway; nothing came of the move (Wetterstedt to Rehausen, Aug. 8, SRA, Anglica; Carl Johan to Carl XIII, Aug. 9, to Frederick William, Aug. 8, to Duke of Mecklenburg-Schwerin, Sept. 29, BFA).

[29] Thornton to Castlereagh, Oct. 17, 1813, London FO, Sweden, 83; Suremain, 315ff; Carl Johan to Blücher, Sept. 29, Oct. 1, 7, BFA; Adlercreutz to Engeström, Oct. 3, Stockholm KB, Engeström Samling.

had left Dresden and with 160,000 troops was advancing straight toward him. The brave Prussians grew hesitant and Blücher himself suggested a postponement of the offensive on Leipzig. Carl Johan agreed. He saw two alternatives: to fall back to the Elbe, or to advance to the Saale and contact the Bohemian Army approaching Leipzig from the south. Blücher now accepted the Saale concentration, and by abandoning his communications and moving quickly evaded Napoleon's blow.[30] By October eleventh both armies lay on the Saale, west and north of Leipzig, and for the first time Blücher was in the more advanced position.

Bernadotte's line of communication was of vastly more importance than was Blücher's, for it was his only means of contact with his own country. When a French rally captured Roslau that line of communication hung entirely on the Elbe-crossing at Acken. Denmark had now declared war and might invade Sweden at any time. And then Bernadotte heard of Napoleon's advance toward Wittenberg. Visioning a trap in his rear, at midnight of October 12-13 he ordered his army to retreat to Cothen, half-way between the Saale and the Elbe. One order stated his intention to strengthen the bridge at Acken and then join Blücher at Halle, but other orders indicated that he meant to cross the Elbe and deflect Napoleon's northward thrust, to save Berlin and his own line of communications. For Bernadotte to make such a

[30] Vincent to Metternich, Oct. 9, 1813, Vienna SA; Carl Johan to Alexander, etc., Oct. 9, SRA, Högkv. Kon.; Schinkel, *Minnen*, VII, 420-421; Carl Johan to Blücher, to Platoff, Oct. 11, BFA.

move alone would have been suicide. But he did not intend to make it alone. He explained his information in a note to Blücher, then *ordered* Blücher to coöperate, saying that the Tsar had permitted him thus to take command in case of necessity. Blücher resented the Prince's assumption of authority: there rankled in his mind his ancient defeat at Lübeck by Marshal Bernadotte, Bernadotte's contempt for the Prussians, his hard use of them in battle, and his super-cautious tactics. Blücher refused to follow and hotly reproached the Prince for threatening to leave the Prussians in their advanced position; obviously he disbelieved Bernadotte's information.[31]

Napoleon's orders, however, substantiate both the information and the intuition of the Prince. Until mid-afternoon of October 12 the Emperor was looking for Bernadotte and Blücher, and almost miraculously his troops had missed Blücher at Düben by half an hour; Napoleon was also seriously considering the march to Magdeburg and Berlin which Bernadotte feared, and had kept his main strength between Düben and Wittenberg. While trying to locate the allied armies, and thinking that Bernadotte must have re-crossed the Elbe, Napoleon heard that the Bohemian Army had come out of the mountains and marched toward Leipzig. Then and then only did he change his plans and go south to meet the greater danger.[32]

[31] See Tingsten, *Huvuddragen* . . . *1813-1814*, 162-170.

[32] *Ibid.*, 172-183; Fain, II, 367-376.

Tingsten doubts that Bernadotte thought Napoleon would march north; indeed, the documents he found do not prove it. However, a letter from Wetterstedt to Engeström and to Toll, leaves little doubt:

"Napoleon, almost surrounded, has, with the greatest part of his army,

Bernadotte's reasoning was absolutely correct, but by accident Blücher's guess proved still more correct.

On October thirteenth when Bernadotte received Blücher's angry letter, neither of them knew where Napoleon was, and did not dream the French were counter-marching to Leipzig. Hence when Carl Johan called a Council of War at Cothen everyone was excited and suspicious. Gneisenau reported evidence of concentration on Leipzig, but Napoleon himself was at Düben until morning of the fourteenth, and Carl Johan still feared for his communications and for Berlin. The allied and Swedish officers pled that the Prince march toward Halle or Leipzig.[33] Bernadotte hesitated, but by eleven in the forenoon of October fourteenth he notified Blücher he would come to Halle. Next day the march started, then halted.

In explanation of his moves Carl Johan related his fears for Berlin, the information about the concentration on Leipzig, and continued:

"J'ai donc pris le parti de me reporter aujourd'hui de Cothen vers Halle. En chemin j'ai reçu par mes agens l'avis qu'une bataille pourra avoir lieu demain. J'ai arrêté ici, à coté de Petersberg et à Zorbig, toutes les troupes sous mes ordres, étant très fatiguées par une marche difficile dans les chemins horribles. Si rien en [ne?] menace mon flanc gauche du coté de la Mulda, je me porterai en avant demain vers Leipzig et je pourrai toujours, avec une

cast himself over the Elbe, and marches now on Berlin. He gives up thus all South Germany and sacrifices his communications with France, but robs us of ours for the moment also. Supposedly he seeks to go home by Magdeburg to Holland. I write this by Cossacks who will seek to break through to tranquilize His Majesty. . . ." (SRA, Högkv. Kon.).
[33] Stewart to Castlereagh, Oct. 17, 1813, London FO, Prussia 90; *Castlereagh Corr.*, IX, 68.

partie de me cavalerie au moins, arriver vers le soir, afin
d'appuyer en cas de besoin les efforts le l'armée combinée,
si la grande bataille s'engage."[34]

The same lack of eagerness for battle was betrayed in
a letter to Blücher, saying "if success is balanced, you
will decide the victory."[35]  No regrets that he could
not be there, no offer to hurry.  He is reported to
have said, "Provided the French are beaten it is indifferent to me whether I or my army take a part,
and of the two, I had much rather we did not."[36]

When Carl Johan halted his troops in the march to
Halle the allied envoys had a meeting and sent a strong
letter praying the Prince to advance and take part in
the inevitable battle.  His own chancellor wrote him
just as strongly:

"Monseigneur:
    Le General Stewart rend compte à Votre Altesse Royale,
de la brillante victoire que le General Blücher vient de
remporter aujourd'hui.  La journée de démain sera plus
décisive encore, si Votre Altesse Royale se porte en avant
avec toute Son Armée, et cela assez à tems pour rencontrer à
l'ennemi, qui est refoulé maintenant vers Leipzig.  Je
réitère à Votre Altesse Royale que les Suédois désirent
d'acquerir de la gloire sous Vos yeux, et que le dicton du
General Suchtelen (qui nous a enlevé Sveaborg, ce que nul
Suédois n'oublie), qu'il doit nous être ni différent par qui
Napoléon est battu, n'est ni moralement, ni politiquement
juste, puisque les Suédois sont ici pour se battre et rougiront

---

[34] Oct. 15, 1813, at Sublitz, BFA.
[35] Oct. 14, 1813, BFA.
[36] *Bath Archives*, II, 311.  At Halle Bernadotte said he would be in the
second line ready to "support if necessary" (*ibid.*, II, 312).

s'ils n'ont pas pu, une fois, convaincre Votre Altesse Royale, qu'ils sont dignes de combattre sous Son commandement."[37]

Bernadotte did move forward, but his ideas remained unfathomable.

For the first day of the Battle of the Nations Carl Johan was not present, though Stewart thought he could have so moved as to destroy the French left wing. The Prince agreed to participate on the eighteenth if Blücher would lend him 30,000 men. He feared Napoleon would attempt to escape toward Berlin and the Elbe forts, and did not wish to be in his path with only the 65,000 men he had left. The Prussian general yielded with ill grace.[38] Swedish infantry did not get into battle until the nineteenth, but Swedish and Prussian artillery took a prominent part on the eighteenth. Slow to act, in battle Bernadotte was always gallant; he led the complaining emissaries into the thickest of the fight. He was bedecked like a knight at a tourney, riding a white charger, and "clad in a tunic of violet velvet braided with gold; on his head, a hat with white feathers, surmounted by an immense plume in the Swedish colors; . . . in his hand his baton covered with violet velvet, ornamented at each end with a gold crown . . . superb thus in the midst of grape-shot, with dead and wounded all about him."[39] On the nineteenth he activated the pursuit of Napoleon, and was among the first to enter Leipzig,

[37] Oct. 16, 1813, SRA, C. J. Papper, 69-3. The letter from the foreign envoys is in Scaevola, 377; see also *ibid.*, 374-377; *Castlereagh Corr.*, IX, 67-68; Schinkel, *Minnen, Bihang*, III, 202.

[38] Stewart to Castlereagh, Oct. 17, 1813, London FO, Prussia 90; Tingsten, *Huvuddragen . . . 1813-1814*, 209-214.

[39] Rochechouart, *Memoirs* (London, 1920), 216.

still clad as if for amateur theatricals. Sovereigns and Prince met joyously in the open square; they had kept the rendezvous of Trachenberg.

The serious question about Bernadotte's movements concerns not his military strategy but his political sincerity. There can hardly be any well-grounded indictment of his movements until October 15, when he halted his troops at Petersberg. That, and his letters to Alexander and Blücher, indicate a real unwillingness to fight. All the allied representatives except Suchtelen agree that he willfully held back. Yet his own position would have been a sad one had Napoleon won at Leipzig, and then pounced on his meager 65,000. Evidently he wished to let the other armies win if they could; they could hold Napoleon for a day at least; then if necessary he would give the decisive blow. He did not wish to be present at a French slaughter, and he was always opposed to the Prussian brute-force tactics; a strategic victory was sufficient for him. His Fabian policy was safe and wise, and although his tactics in the last days erred it was from the accident of events rather than false premises. His slowness of movement was due not to treachery but to open distaste for his task and over-driven cautiousness.

Despite the stench of unburied dead horses and men the monarchs stayed in Leipzig several days. Unfortunately most of the time was frittered away in petty questions, while the matter of a permanent alliance had to wait. Agreement was reached about the organization of new-won territory, and the distribution of the "contributions" therefrom. Tsar and Crown Prince conversed on personal and European questions, but mystery shrouds the results; we know only that the Prince was unhappy.[40]

On the matter of the subsidy renewal Thornton and the Swedes reached an agreement at Leipzig. Early in the summer the Swedes had asked for a renewal treaty, but although the Cabinet in August authorized renewal, Castlereagh delayed sending instructions until late in September so that there could be no question of a first of October payment. The real difficulty was in the amount Sweden asked. Wetterstedt said the army cost 150,000 pounds per month and Sweden could pay none of it because of the additional expense of her reserve army in Skåne.[41] Sweden was indeed in a critical financial situation, and her Riksdag was not at all likely to vote money for a war in Germany, allied with Russia; the state no longer reaped huge revenues from the Falun copper mine as in the days of Gustavus Adolphus and Charles XII. A forced loan on the merchants of Gothenburg had been paid, but with such an attitude that repetition was decidedly unwise.[42] Castlereagh nevertheless thought Sweden should bear some of the expense and therefore offered 100,000 pounds per month for a maximum of twelve months campaigning. Wetterstedt wrote angrily to

[40] Schück, *Skjöldebrands Memoarer*, V, 60; Löwenhielm to Carl Johan, Nov. 2, 1813, enclosing copies of the convention of Oct. 21, and Löwenhielm's letter to Hardenberg of Oct. 22 acceding to this Austro-Russo-Prussian agreement, SRA. Sweden was to get one-seventeenth of the proceeds of the "contributions."

[41] Wetterstedt to Rehausen, July 22, 1813, SRA, Anglica; to Wirsén, July 13, SRA, Wirsén Samling.

[42] Carl Johan to Rosen (Governor of Gothenburg), Mar. 8, 1813, BFA; Rosen to Engeström, Mar. 13, 26, Stockholm KB, Engeström Samling; to Wirsén, Apr. 5, SRA, Wirsén Sam.

London that this was not a continuation but a reduction, that Sweden needed 150,000 pounds and had been led to expect it; she accepted from loyalty to the common cause but the army would have to retire to Sweden's mountains when the funds ran out.[43]

This financial disappointment touched the Prince in a sensitive spot, and, added to the suspicions and recriminations before Leipzig, left in his heart a resentment which was to contribute to the independent action on which he soon embarked.

[43] Castlereagh to Thornton, Sept. 24, 1813, London FO, Sweden 80; Rehausen to Wetterstedt, Sept. 14, 16, Wetterstedt to Rehausen, Oct. 22, SRA, Anglica; Wetterstedt to Thornton, Oct. 22, SRA, Högkv. Kon.; Thornton to Castlereagh, Oct. 22, London FO, Sweden 83. The agreement is in *British and Foreign State Papers*, I, 296ff.

## VI

## The Danish Campaign and Austrian Intrigue

### *November 1813 to January 1814*

BERNADOTTE felt that Leipzig had released him: his obligation to the allies was paid. He might now turn to Swedish business, crush Davoust at Hamburg and wrest Norway from Denmark. For a few days he followed along in the ineffective pursuit of the French, but on October 29 redirected the Swedish army toward Hanover, and announced that he would restore Hanover to its legitimate ruler, collect fresh troops, cut off Davoust's retreat, and open communication with England. In Hanover, where Bernadotte the marshal had left a reputation for efficient and courteous government, he conferred with both British and Hanoverian ministers about the new government. This annoyed rather than pleased the British, who wanted Carl Johan in Holland; the Prussians despised him for evading the main struggle; Alexander wanted him nearby to realize on any opportunity for overthrowing Napoleon. Only the Austrians were happy at the departure of the hated and distrusted Gascon.

Although Bernadotte stopped to reorganize Hanover and to suggest Hanoverian or Swedish protectorates over the Hanseatic cities [1] his vital concern was Nor-

---

[1] Wetterstedt to Engeström, Oct. 28, 1813, SRA; Thornton to Castlereagh, Oct. 28, London FO, Sweden 84.

way. He realized that since his services were no longer indispensable he would find it increasingly difficult to get allied support. The despoliation of Denmark was distasteful to all the allies, and the Austrians were doing their best to scuttle the Swedish program. The Austrian refusal to mention Norway in the treaties of Teplitz (Sept. 9, 1813) led even Stewart to suggest that no one knew "what necessity might bring about at a general arrangement."[2] Precisely this attitude made Bernadotte anxious to get actual possession of Norway at once, especially since the Danish declaration of war (Sept. 3) and Christian Frederick's activities in Norway.

Early in November G. Löwenhielm was sent to general headquarters to argue that the attack on Davoust and the Danes was a necessary defensive step, and would really hasten the conquest of Holland. Alexander showed little surprise,[3] but on November 10 sent back a plan utterly different, one to which the Austrian and Prussian military men had agreed. The scheme was to close in on Paris as they had closed in on Leipzig: Wellington's army should advance from Spain, the Austrian army from Italy, and the main army through Switzerland; Blücher should operate along the Rhine, and Bernadotte invade Holland. There was no hint of military action against Denmark, but the Tsar claimed Austria would either bring her into the coalition or break relations. Alexander called this an answer to Carl Johan's request at Leipzig; he

---

[2] *Bath Archives*, II, 277.

[3] Instructions for G. Löwenhielm, undated, G. Löwenhielm to Carl Johan, Nov. 7, 1813, SRA, G. L. Sam.

felt sure the Prince would do all for a cause which was his, that of the liberty of peoples, and of all humanity.[4]

Dramatic scenes at Swedish headquarters must have followed receipt (Nov. 12-13) of the Tsar's *"plan gigantesque."* Were the suggestions of Bernadotte, author of the victorious Trachenberg Plan, to be discarded by three mere sovereigns for the scheme of *"faiseurs"* like Gneisenau and the Austrians? Were the claims to Norway to be thwarted once more? Not this time, for Bernadotte was now in a position to act while he argued. At once he both put his army in motion and sent out his emissaries. To Copenhagen he sent Kammerherre Hedeman on an abortive mission offering again the terms of May.[5] To Hamburg he sent Herr Meyer to appeal to Davoust to surrender. And to the allied headquarters he sent both Gustav Löwenhielm and his right-hand man Wetterstedt, laden with voluminous instructions and observations. Wetterstedt's primary objects were to gain allied sanction for the military moves on which Carl Johan had already embarked and to persuade the powers to set aside specific territories as indemnities which could be promised to Denmark for Norway.

Carl Johan pledged aid to the common cause but insisted again on the danger of leaving Denmark and as many as 130,000 French troops in the rear in masked garrisons. In the winter, he mentioned, the Danes might be able to invade Sweden over the ice. The

[4] Schinkel, *Minnen, Bihang,* III, 214-216, and cf., Schinkel, *Minnen,* VII, 298.

[5] See below, p. 134. On Bernadotte's deliberately independent policy see, e.g., his orders to Benningsen of Nov. 8, 1813, BFA (incomplete in *Recueil,* 452-454); Tingsten, *Huvuddragen . . . 1813-1814,* 265 note.

headquarters plan meant campaigning in enemy territory, where the French nation would rise *en masse*
and destroy an army even of 600,000 such as Napoleon
had taken to Moscow. Even Wellington, "one of the
first captains of our century," had awaited the fall of
San Sebastian before invading France. The Swedish
forces could take Holland and attack the borders of
France, but first they must defeat Davoust and the
Danes. Premature invasion would rouse republicanism
in France and create an opportunity for a Polish revolt.
The way must be prepared by a proclamation guaran-
teeing France her natural boundaries and proving that
the allies fought everywhere for the liberty of peoples.
Napoleon must be put in the wrong by rejecting fair
terms of peace and France then should have the chance
to decide between the allies and Napoleon. "If these
principles are not followed the present coalition will be
destroyed as the others."[6]

While Wetterstedt was on his way Castlereagh was
praising Bernadotte in the House of Commons for his
magnanimity in advancing on Holland. This was a
little previous. On November 16, the day after Wetterstedt left, the Prince directed most of his army
northeast toward Denmark, and after a moment of
hesitation in Bremen he decided that he must lead
that army in person.[7] Down at the main headquarters
the Tsar decided not to be disagreeable about a *fait
accompli*; he gave his blessing to the move and only

[6] "Military Observation," Nov. 15, 1813, SRA, Högkv. Kon.; Schinkel,
*Minnen,* VII, 423-429; Wetterstedt's instructions, Nov. 14, SRA, Wetterstedts SB.

[7] Thornton to Castlereagh, Nov. 19, 1813, and Feb. 17, 1814, London
FO, Sweden 84 and 90 respectively; Webster, *Castlereagh,* 181-182.

reminded the Swedes of the need to hurry to Holland. He agreed that a proclamation should precede the invasion of France; it was being worked out. Even Metternich and the King of Prussia were gracious to the Swedish chancellor, whom they considered the "most sensible and pleasant man of the whole Swedish party."[8]

On the problem of specifying indemnities for Denmark Wetterstedt was less successful. Sweden would exchange Guadeloupe for some less valuable Danish colony, and would cede Pomerania, but beyond this the problem grew complex. Saxe-Lauenburg was suggested, and the Tsar's mentions of Mecklenburg-Schwerin, and protectorates over Hamburg and Lübeck were declared satisfactory. However, the use of German territories necessitated compensation to the present or past rulers, and into this labyrinth of exchanges the allies absolutely refused to enter. When Bernadotte saw the situation and agreed to cede Pomerania only to Prussia, which coveted it, he gained one helper. But one was not enough, so Swedish persistence availed nothing.[9]

Besides these questions of campaign plans and territorial exchanges Wetterstedt at once found himself face to face with an amazing array of new problems. Sir Charles Stewart, who went with Wetterstedt to

[8] Wetterstedt to Carl Johan, Nov. 22, 1813, G. Löwenhielm to Carl Johan, Nov. 24, SRA; Alexander to Carl Johan, Nov. 24, 29, SRA, Främ. Suv.; Bath Archives, II, 370.

[9] Wetterstedt to Carl Johan, Nov. 22 et seq., 1813, SRA; Wirsén to Wetterstedt, Nov. 27, 30, Schulzenheim to Wetterstedt, Nov. 30, Dec. 2, 4, Carl Johan to Wetterstedt, Dec. 1, SRA, Wetterstedts S.B.; Wetterstedt to Wirsén, Dec. 4, SRA, Wirsén Samling.

Frankfort, had just received news of the peace proposals made by the allies to Napoleon through Baron St. Aignan. Stewart was furious at the secrecy of the step, both on his own account and on that of Bernadotte, who should be kept *au courant* even if he were difficult; he had "some great qualities" and his name held a "certain magic which we must see the effects of properly to appreciate."[10] Wetterstedt soon found that Löwenhielm and Bildt knew nothing, and when he demanded explanations he got only excuses and apologies from Alexander, Nesselrode, Hardenberg, Metternich. The proposals were only unofficial bases, but bases were important and secrecy was dangerous. These bases were silent on Norway and on other vital points. Of Metternich's farsighted scheming Bernadotte was innately suspicious, and it was as fortunate for him as for Great Britain that these bases were not quickly accepted.[11]

A further source of friction was the permanent alliance against France which Castlereagh had proposed in September. In the original plan Sweden was included along with Great Britain, Russia, Prussia, and Austria, though she might "accede" rather than sign. The Bernadotte-hating Cathcart had charge of the negotiations, and held up proceedings until he could confer with Alexander. After October 25, with the

[10] Stewart to Castlereagh, Nov. 15, 1813, London FO, Prussia 91. Evidently Stewart received Jackson's letter on Nov. 15 and discussed it with Bernadotte, but did not disclose the matter to Wetterstedt until they were *en route* (C. K. Webster, *British Diplomacy 1813-1815* [London, 1921], 87-93; Wirsén to his wife, Nov. 15, SRA, Wirsén Samling).

[11] Webster, *Castlereagh*, 166-184; Wetterstedt to Carl Johan, Nov. 22, 24, Dec. 2, 4, 1813, SRA; Rehausen to Wetterstedt, Dec. 17, SRA, Anglica; Metternich to Bildt, Dec. 6, Vienna SA.

Tsar's authorization, the question was opened with Metternich and later with Hardenberg. It was not mentioned officially to the Swedes because opposition to their inclusion appeared immediately. Who started it? When Cathcart wrote on October 30, "It is not wished to make the communication in the first instance to Sweden, but rather to propose to that power to accede," was he stating a suggestion from Alexander? Or was he expressing rather his own and Metternich's and Aberdeen's open distrust of Bernadotte? Certainly if Alexander did thus early turn against his Gascon friend, Cathcart was delighted to support him, as were Metternich and Aberdeen and Nesselrode.[12]

Unfortunately for good feeling Thornton, exasperated with the delay, had broached the subject to Wetterstedt. When Löwenhielm then asked Cathcart about the "Quintuple Alliance" the British envoy had to lie: he had not heard of a "Quintuple Alliance" (that *term* had not been used) and if there had been such an idea it had probably been dropped.[13] When Wetterstedt reached headquarters he saw things clearly, and was exasperated that the allies should ask the Prince to adapt his moves to their interests and at the same time treat behind his back. Cathcart stood by his guns, rebuking Stewart—any overture to Sweden was "premature, unauthorized and tending to inter-

---

[12] Webster, *British Diplomacy*, 19-29, 35-36; Stewart to Castlereagh, Oct. 21, London FO, Prussia 90. Professor Webster believes Alexander specifically asked the exclusion of Sweden, but the writer cannot but think that Cathcart, Aberdeen and Metternich were the prime movers in this suggestion (Webster, *Castlereagh*, 160, 168, 177-178; Webster, *British Diplomacy*, 41-55).

[13] Cathcart to Castlereagh, Nov. 17, 1813 (private), London FO, Supplement (Russia) 343.

rupt the harmony subsisting among the allies."[14]  Carl Johan was already alarmingly "disharmonized"; he knew the exclusion was aimed directly at him, and it did little good for Castlereagh to explain that the burdens of the alliance would probably be more than Sweden would wish to assume.[15]

Wetterstedt and Löwenhielm had got approval for the Swedish military plans, and had wormed out a little information on the Frankfort peace proposals. On the indemnities they had gained nothing, and on the new alliance they met an impenetrable fog of silence and deceit. With the "sordid greed" of the allies and their "impertinent" claim to be *grandes puissances* they could not cope. A new nobility of might among the nations was forcing Sweden and her Prince into a subservient rôle. With these bitter thoughts Wetterstedt returned in mid-December over the wintry road from Frankfort to Kiel, complaining as he went that Carl Johan's victories had doubled the length of his journey.[16]

The day after Wetterstedt had started on his futile mission, Bernadotte had sent Bülow and Winzingerode toward Holland, while he led 60,000 men to the northeast. General Wallmoden's repeated advice convinced him that he could not capture Hamburg or defeat Davoust's force without using his entire army and consuming much time. A way out seemed to offer

[14] To Stewart, Nov. 30, 1813, London FO, Prussia, 91.

[15] Castlereagh to Thornton, Dec. 17, 1813, London FO, Sweden 80; H. T. Colenbrander, *Gedenkstukken der Algemeene Geschiedenis van Nederland van 1795 tot 1840 . . . VII Deel, 1813-1815* (The Hague, 1914), XXIII, 16-18; on Bernadotte's attitude see Thornton's despatch of Dec. 16 (secret), London FO, Sweden 84.

[16] Schulzenheim to Engeström, Dec. 18, 1813, SRA, Högkv. Kon.

when Karl Sieveking, one of his Hamburg admirers since the spring, came again begging aid. It was probably Bernadotte himself who suggested a secret mission to Davoust, offering for the surrender of Hamburg to allow the French troops to return home with no obligation against future service; Davoust's Dutch and Hanseatic soldiers should be released, and property left intact.

Sieveking evidently did not relish the mission for himself, but sent a Herr Meyer of Altona. He told Meyer that Bernadotte was willing to make this offer out of regard for Hamburg and because he was "repugnant to spill the blood of Frenchmen when the great cause of the independence of peoples does not imperiously require it." St. Cyr at Dresden, he continued, had considered his troops more useful on the Moselle than on the Elbe and had made a similar agreement with General Klenau, although the allies later disavowed it. This arrangement would advantage both Davoust and Bernadotte, whose policy, *"si elle y entre, n'y gagne pas aux depens de la France."* Meyer reached Hamburg on November 19 and that evening was allowed a long talk with the testy old marshal, now Prince d'Eckmühl. Despite Meyer's arguments and the marshal's foreboding of inevitable ruin he declaimed that he would defend himself to the last in the smoking débris of Hamburg. Sieveking could only report that royalty had had its martyrs, and republics too; now Davoust evidently wished tyranny to have its turn.[17]

[17] Sieveking to Meyer, Nov. 17, 1813, to Carl Johan, Nov. 21, Upsala, Alin Samling, XIII. Since my study of this incident a thorough account

In his offer to Davoust Bernadotte acted openly, not treacherously, yet he directly repudiated the decision of his allies who had, in denouncing the capitulation agreement at Dresden, indicated clearly a preference to mask French garrisons rather than to allow them to return home and form the nuclei for new French levies. Bernadotte wrote the Tsar about his offer, and discussed it with the allied representatives. Sir Charles Stewart strongly opposed the plan, and Wallmoden did not state his opinion clearly. Thornton and, strange to say, the Austrian Vincent, approved of the scheme. They admitted it would strengthen Napoleon's army in France, but thought it more important to relieve the still larger body of allied besieging forces, which would hasten the collapse of Denmark and enable Bernadotte to get to Holland more quickly.[18] Bernadotte personally was very likely influenced by feelings of humanity, by sentiment and policy toward France, and above all by a desire to get immediate and firm control of German territory which would assure Denmark of indemnities for Norway.

With the failure of negotiations a large army was thrown around Hamburg and the remaining forces marched on to Denmark. By December 5 the Russo-Swedish forces had occupied Lübeck and advanced

of it has been published: T. T. Höjer, "Carl Johans Kapitulationsanbud till Davoust," *Karl Johan Förbundets Handlingar* (1931-1934), 1-29.

[18] Schulzenheim to Rehausen, Nov. 26, 1813, SRA, Anglica; *Castlereagh Corr.*, IX, 76-78; Carl Johan to Alexander, Nov. 15, BFA. Cf., Webster, *Castlereagh*, 188. According to Thiébault's *Mémoires* (V, 182ff) Bernadotte sent also to Davoust an émigré restaurauteur named Rainville, who at first sight of the gruff old soldier stammered some platitudes and fled; the tale may be discarded, for not even Pingaud accepts it (*Bernadotte, Napoléon et les Bourbons*, [Paris, 1901], 256ff).

into Holstein. Bernadotte at once levied a "contri-
bution" of 1,000,000 riksdalers, anxious that neither
Holstein nor the rich Hanse cities should be brought
under Stein's central Council.[19]  The conquest of Denmark proceeded rapidly, unspectacularly, the march
of overwhelming forces against heroic but out-classed
Danish recruits.

In December the drama of diplomacy grew more and
more complex, with the Austrian chief minister as the
villain of the piece.

Metternich's half-hearted warning to Bernstorff early
in October had had no effect because it had not been
sent to Denmark.  At Leipzig Metternich had promised a direct *démarche*, but he had postponed it week
after week.  At last the Austrian Count Bombelles
started for Copenhagen November 16, perhaps then
only because Wetterstedt was about to arrive at headquarters.  Metternich had promised that his propositions would conform to Sweden's May demands and
that Bombelles would show his instructions to Carl
Johan.  Instead, these instructions specifically required
the emissary to avoid Swedish headquarters and go
through Berlin, and he traveled incognito as his servant's servant.  The reason is obvious, for the instructions read:

"L'Empereur croit pouvoir offrir ses bons offices au Danemarc pour modifier ces bases [the Swedish demands] aux
conditions suivantes, savoir: la cession immediate du baillage

[19] Schulzenheim to Wetterstedt, Dec. 7, 1813, SRA, Högkv. Kon.;
Wirsén to Wetterstedt, Dec. 2, and drafts of Dec. 18, and Jan. 3, 1814,
SRA, Wirsén Samling.

de Drontheim [Trondhjem] sans un engagement quelconque qui porterait sur le reste de la Norvège.

"L'Autriche s'engage donc à interposer ses bons offices pour que la Norvége à l'exception du Drontheim soit garantie par les puissances alliées au Danemarc. Elles chercheraient les moyens les plus aptes pour indemniser le Danemarc pour la perte de Drontheim. La paix avec l'Angleterre sur les bases les plus libérales; l'admission à la grande alliance seraient les suites immediates de l'accord, qui s'etablirait entre le Danemarc et les puissances alliées."

Bombelles was then to threaten breaking off relations if Denmark refused this basis; if she accepted the terms Bombelles would write to Wallmoden urging an armistice (not to Carl Johan!); he would also send an enclosed letter to Castlereagh.[20]

The evening of Bombelles' arrival in Copenhagen (November 27, 1813), Lutzow, Austrian Minister, took him to the eager Rosenkrantz. The Danish Minister's hope congealed at mention of Trondhjem; the King would not cede a single village. When Bombelles replied that this meant the fall of a monarchy Rosenkrantz at length agreed to advise the cession, and he looked more confident when the envoy continued,

". . . que les chances de l'avenir étaient incalculables, qu'une cession n'était pas toujours éternelle, et que le Danemarc, une fois ramené aux vrais principes, pourrait, s'il le voulait, grandement balancer l'amitié des puissances alliées pour la Suède."[21]

Rosenkrantz grasped both the necessities of the immediate situation and the possibilities of future retraction.

---

[20] Y. Nielsen, *Aktmaessige Bidrag til de nordiske Rigers politiske Historie i 1813 og 1814* (Christiania, 1877), 46.

[21] Bombelles' report to Metternich, Nielsen, *op. cit.*, 49.

The stubborn, slow-minded King Frederick, however, turned his back when Rosenkrantz mentioned the demands. Exaggerated ideas of Danish strength and of Napoleon's ability and generosity made him spurn the most liberal proposal of months, a proposal meant to save Denmark from ruin, one which Metternich would have to force down Bernadotte's throat.

At length Rosenkrantz got Frederick to call a council of chief officials. Although they only half understood the catastrophe that stared them in the face their memoranda gave a sad picture of Denmark's military and financial plight. Rosenkrantz wished to hedge. He would state Denmark's demands (restoration of colonies and fleet) and *talk* of the cession of Trondhjem; actual cession he would avoid by refusing every compensation offered. Or it might be "safer and more honorable" not to mention Trondhjem, but to offer orally to negotiate on proposals from Austria. Denmark might "adjust the Norwegian boundary" but cession of a whole province might lead to the early loss of all Norway. Swedish shipping damages could be compensated by granting Sweden freedom from the Sound dues. In sum, Denmark must make the best of a bad situation.[22] One of the other statesmen would "meet the enemy at the border." Another said Napoleon could not help, so territory had to be ceded; honor did not forbid, for the King's ancestors had often done the same! Almost all were opposed to the cession, and though many favored abandoning the French alliance they did not wish to join the coalition.[23]

[22] *Meddelelser*, VII, 409-412; Friis, *Nye Akstykker*, 13-19.
[23] The memoranda of Dec. 2-5 are in Friis, *op. cit.*, 19-42.

An armistice at least was essential and Bombelles assured the dubious Danes that Carl Johan and his 18,000 [!] Swedes could not prevent it. Confirmation of the Austrian claims seemed to be given by Aberdeen's eagerness for Danish accession to the alliance, and reports that the British Ministry regretted its promises to Sweden. King Frederick wrote his general, Prince Frederick of Hesse, to get an armistice on the pretext that peace proposals had been made; Davoust should be included if he wished, but Denmark at least must have a respite. Then this letter, making patent the insincerity of the armistice request, was intercepted and sent to Carl Johan.[24]

Still the King would not receive Bombelles or reply to the Austrian points. On December 4 the envoy said he would depart in forty-eight hours if he did not get a categorical response. Rosenkrantz pled but could not change him, and at last with tears in his eyes promised to join the coalition, but was there not something besides Trondhjem to satisfy Carl Johan? Bombelles lowered his eyes and said the conditions were unalterable. By next day the King received Bombelles in audience.[25]

The following day another special council was held, and the memoranda for it showed a degree of resignation to fate, and advised placing Denmark's trust in Austria and hoping for the best. Again, a councillor advised promising Trondhjem orally while retaining it

[24] *Ibid.*, 13-17; Fred. VI to Fred. of Hesse, Dec. 4, 1813, copy sent to Löwenhielm by Wetterstedt, Dec. 14, SRA, Musc.

[25] Friis, *Nye Aktstykker*, 44-46; Nielsen, *Akt. Bidrag . . . 1813-1814*, 55-60.

under whatever excuses arose.[26]  After the meeting the King accepted the Austrian basis of transfer of Denmark to the coalition, and cession of Trondhjem to Sweden against indemnities to be obtained through Austrian mediation.  In his letter to Prince Christian Frederick, Statholder of Norway, the King emphasized the oral character of the pledge and ended:

"it may be avoided if the people of Trondhjem say 'we will remain with our King,' above all we can win time and get the Allies certainly on our side now that the Crown Prince is known to them all as a braggart and a cruel, base man.  You can realize what I feel and what it all is for me, and that I think of nothing else than to get it back again."[27]

These short-sighted mental reservations were to lead to sad results.

Bombelles, elated at his seeming success, sent off his letters to Wallmoden and to Wessenberg.  But Metternich had not been quite clever enough.  Carl Johan had led his campaign in person; hence Wallmoden had no right to conclude an armistice, but sent the letter to the Prince and continued his campaign. The duchies were invaded and Bombelles wrote again to Wallmoden.  Still he got no reply.  His letters to Wessenberg and Castlereagh said Denmark had accepted the Austrian demands *in toto*, and asked for an armistice at sea and the despatch of grain boats to Norway.  Wessenberg and the British, however, recognized that the Austrian terms were not the Swedish demands, and would do nothing until they had official

[26] Memoranda in Friis, *op. cit.*, 47-59.
[27] Dec. 7, 1813, Sørensen, *Kampen om Norge*, I, 403-404; *Meddelelser*, IX, 131-132.

word of a land armistice.[28] How could Metternich have expected them to do otherwise, with the example of the Dolgorouki mission still in mind? Perhaps he counted too much on Aberdeen's influence.

The peace activity begun by the King on December 4 led to an exchange of notes between Frederick of Hesse and Carl Johan and through this to an armistice on December 15. The armies were to remain in position and the siege of the Danish forts continue during a two weeks respite. Carl Johan understood the duplicity of Frederick's proposal, yet hoped Austria would force Denmark to terms.[29]

Colonel Hedeman, the Dane who for a month had been carrying peace proposals between Bernadotte's headquarters and the Danish lines, finally realized the futility of his well-meant endeavors, and was allowed to depart with the Prince's blessing; his activity only illustrates the persistence of Bernadotte's diplomacy.[30] King Frederick refused to receive Hedeman, and at the same time ordered Bernstorff to proceed to Austrian headquarters and obstruct Bernadotte's program.

[28] Bombelles to Wallmoden, Dec. 7, 1813, Wallmoden to Bombelles, Dec. 21 (a tardy acknowledgment, no more), Bombelles to Wessenberg, Dec. 7, Wessenberg to Bombelles, Dec. 23 (copies), Rehausen to Wetterstedt, Jan. 4, 1814, SRA, Freden i Kiel; see also in Lund, de la Gardie Samling, I, 191-194; Rehausen to Wetterstedt Dec. 23, SRA, Anglica; *Castlereagh Corr.*, IX, 107-109.

[29] Charles of Hesse to Wallmoden, Dec. 8, 1813, Frederick of Hesse to Carl Johan, Dec. 9, 11, Carl Johan to Frederick of Hesse, Dec. 9 *et seq.*, BFA.

[30] Original of Hedeman's report, Dec. 16, 1813, is in Upsala, Schinkel Samling VI. Another long memorandum, with some documents, is printed (*Meddelelser*, IX, 118-130, and 7-10). According to this Hedeman was charged by the Prince to tell King Frederick he was "*un sot et un imbécile.*"

Rosenkrantz wrote Bernstorff on December 7 revealing anew the Danish scheme:

"Il s'agit de detourner l'effêt de la promesse eventuelle [of the cession of Trondhjem] en rejettant l'indemnité que l'on va nous offrir et qui n'a point encore été articulée. Tout nous fait espérer que l'Autriche ne demande pas mieux que de s'y prêter et nous nous flattons aussi, que ses alliés, surtout l'Angleterre, seconderont nos vues. . . ."[31]

Denmark's game was to keep her sails hoisted until a favorable breeze blew her way. Hence not until December 20 did she send Kammerherre Bourke as emissary to Carl Johan. Although he was accompanied by Herr Krabbe and the reluctant Bombelles he had power only to ask an extension of the armistice, and inclusion in it of the Danish forts; Denmark merely wanted time to get strong Austrian support in her negotiations with Sweden.[32]

Baron Tawast meantime was sent to Copenhagen by Bernadotte, without power to treat, but carrying the latest edition of peace proposals: now all Norway was inalterably required, but only Trondhjem and the two forts need be ceded at once; for immediate possession of Norway 1,000,000 riksdalers would be granted; hope was held out for quick peace between Denmark and Great Britain, Russia and Prussia. Rosenkrantz could not agree to such terms even as a basis, despite Tawast's offer to prolong the armistice for negotiations. After an angry nine day exchange of notes Tawast left Copenhagen, December 31, pow-

---

[31] Friis, *Nye Aktstykker*, 60-61, 63-66.
[32] *Ibid.*, 71-73; Nielsen, *op. cit.*, 64-66; *Meddelelser*, IX, 10-12; Rosenkrantz to Bernstorff, Dec. 21, DRA, Geh. Reg.

erless against the Danish insistence on waiting for Austrian encouragement.[33]

At Swedish headquarters in Kiel Bombelles was learning that Suchtelen and Thornton did not see through the same anti-Swedish eyes as did Nesselrode and Aberdeen. He found himself too under suspicion by Wetterstedt and Bernadotte, and made matters worse by writing Vincent that the Emperor would view with favor all he could do for the Danish King.[34] The Danes with whom Bombelles came exasperated the Prince also by having no powers to treat. Bernadotte felt sure Denmark would have accepted his terms but for Austria's interference, and wrote the Emperor Francis straight-forwardly saying that Austria had modified the Swedish demands and that now, because of the allies' refusal to discuss indemnities and his own military success, he must have all of Norway with no alternative about German territory. He concluded,

"Je suis persuadé que le Gouvernement Danois cédera aux efforts et aux représentations des Alliés, s'il ne s'apperçoit pas d'aucune divergence d'opinion à son égard. S'il réussit au contraire à jetter entre nous des semences de discorde et de désunion, il retardera pour sûr la décision, et un tems precieux sera alors perdu, pour la cause générale. . . ."[35]

Because of this resentment against Austria it took seventeen hours of obstinate debate to persuade Bernadotte to grant an armistice extension to January 5,

[33] Instruction for Tawast, Dec. 17, 1813, SRA, Högkv. Kon.; Friis, *op. cit.*, 66f, 74, 76f, 88ff; Tawast to Carl Johan, and to Wetterstedt, Dec. 23 *et seq.*, SRA, Freden i Kiel.

[34] Wetterstedt to Bildt, Dec. 23, 1813, SRA, Högkv. Kon.; Bildt to Wetterstedt, Dec. 22, SRA, Freden i Kiel, and Dec. 25, SRA.

[35] Dec. 26, 1813, SRA, Högkv. Kon.

1814.  Immediately thereafter Bourke went to Schleswig and awaited orders.  Bombelles hastened to Copenhagen, and with clever flattery and depiction of the ruin of war he brought the antagonistic King to calm acceptance of the inevitable.  Bombelles boasted that in two hours he had done what four powerful states had failed to do in a year.  He too brought the old alternatives: (1) immediate cession of Trondhjem and the forts of Kongsvinger and Fredrikshald, with later cession of the rest of Norway, and Danish aid to the coalition, in return for which the Swedes would evacuate Schleswig and Holstein and use their good offices for further indemnities; or (2) immediate cession of all Norway with a financial adjustment for Denmark.[36]

Frederick did not, of course, frankly accept either proposition.  Bernadotte had promised that if indemnities were not found for Denmark he would be *"aussi delicat pour renoncer à la prise de la possession du reste de Norvège."*  Building on this and on his irrepressible hopes Frederick and his council agreed only to cede Trondhjem at once in return for indemnities, the cession of the rest of Norway to be dependent on compensation *acceptable to Denmark.*  Evidently he counted on popular loyalty to his house, and hoped still to protract negotiations until fortune smiled.[37]  The Crown Prince was astonished when Bourke returned to Kiel with these meager concessions.  Holstein he now occupied and Jutland lay helpless before him; he

---

[36] To Metternich, Jan. 1, 1814, Nielsen, *op. cit.*, 66-72.

[37] Nielsen, *op. cit.*, 74, 75; Rosenkrantz to Bourke, Dec. 31, 1813, DRA, Geh. Reg.  These instructions to Bourke are not given by the *Meddelelser* or Friis.

could hardly be expected to be so magnanimous now as to allow Denmark to accept or reject the compensation the allies might offer for the loss of southern Norway. For three weeks Danish vacillation had held the Prince's large army inactive while the allies demanded his advance on France. Hence Bourke was given his passports and hostilities were resumed, January 6, 1814.

Denmark had been playing the only game it was possible to play after her mistakes of the spring. She must delay, for her only hope lay in a general peace negotiation at which allied discontent with Bernadotte's tactics and pretensions would react in Denmark's favor. Such discontent was becoming indeed ominous for the Swedish Prince.

Great Britain was loyal to her pledges but no longer cordial. She wished Carl Johan to support the rising in Holland, and resented his detour to secure his own interests. He was frankly reluctant to go to Holland to destroy what as a soldier of the revolution he had helped to create,[38] and the troops he had sent there were too meager to take the offensive. Stewart even imagined Bernadotte wished to allow Davoust to escape to Holland.[39] The attack on Denmark had been from the first distasteful to most Englishmen, and a number of petty disputes disturbed British-Swedish friendship: the subsidies contention, disagreements on German affairs, provisioning of the island of Anholt, complaints about the British blockade of Norway, and

[38] Webster, *Castlereagh*, 181-182; Renier, *op. cit.*, ch. i. Bernadotte did at least write to Horenken, von Alberda and Möderman to encourage the nationalist rising in the Netherlands (Dec. 1, 1813, BFA).

[39] To Castlereagh, Dec. 20, 1813, London FO, Prussia 91.

occasional diatribes against Bernadotte in the British press.  Feelings thus sensitized were chafed even by a clumsy attempt of Castlereagh to flatter Bernadotte into action in order to "make himself dear to the English nation."  Engeström thought this was insolent egoism—"did the Prince of Wales wish likewise to make himself dear to the Swedish nation?"[40]

Personal antagonism and suspicion continually hounded the former Frenchman.  George Jackson expressed the reason for it after seeing the Prince at Leipzig:

"A more complete Frenchman [Bernadotte] both in appearance and manners I never beheld.  One wonders what business he has amongst us. . . .  His sympathy with our cause evidently goes no further than as its success favours his own private views.  A little relaxation of Bonaparte's obstinacy in that direction would, I feel convinced, have secured his alliance."[41]

Jackson remembered seeing Bernadotte at the head of a French army in 1807.  Still less could the Prussians and Austrians forget that Bernadotte had originated in the enemy camp.  They could not rid their minds of suspicion and their attitude drove the Gascon toward independent action.  Eventually Bernadotte's pent-up wrath exploded.  Why, he demanded, should he be condemned for seeking his own and Sweden's ends?  Was not a ruler's first duty to his people?  As for Holland, he declared Napoleon would not defend it anyway.  Sweden had repeatedly moderated her policy, but if allied chicanery and injustices continued she

[40] Engeström to Carl Johan, Dec. 17, 1813, SRA.
[41] *Bath Archives*, II, 316-317.

might have to abandon the cause she had helped to found.[42]

The discontent of the allies had expressed itself in the joint Russo-Prusso-Austrian mission of Pozzo di Borgo to London in December. He had gone because the three British representatives at headquarters could not coöperate, and the allies wanted at hand one authoritative British statesman who could make decisions. For Bernadotte no more unwelcome messenger could have been chosen. The ambitious Corsican, recently named general by the Tsar and followed everywhere now by a picturesque and thieving Calmuk, was Bernadotte's inveterate enemy. When he left for London the offended Stewart sent Jackson to counteract Pozzo's probable evil work.[43]

As Wetterstedt soon ascertained, Pozzo was to urge Britain to join in excluding small states from the permanent alliance, because of the "inconveniences which would result from this useless complication." Bernadotte should have just enough troops to subdue Denmark, the instructions read, but if Denmark accepted the Austrian terms, Alexander and his allies would force Sweden also to accept these terms.[44] By now the Tsar was certainly supporting an anti-Bernadotte policy. Pozzo got Castlereagh to go to the continent as Britain's representative; he also got British approval of the Austrian terms to Denmark, and of the allied program toward Sweden. This program, involving a clear-cut

[42] Schulzenheim to Rehausen, Feb. 7, 1814, SRA, Anglica.

[43] Webster, *Castlereagh*, 176ff; F. Balfour, *Aberdeen*, I, 161ff; *Bath Archives*, II, 382, 384; Stewart to Castlereagh, Dec. 7, 1813, London FO, Prussia 91.

[44] Nov. 24/Dec. 6, 1813, Upsala, Alin Samling XII.

distinction between great powers and small, and stimulated largely by suspicion of Bernadotte, determined the procedure at the Congress of Châtillon and established a precedent of far-reaching significance.

Rehausen was terrified lest Sweden be excluded from the peace negotiations, but was innocently content when Castlereagh said that he himself was going to the continent. Bernadotte, more and more worried about the mischief Pozzo might do, on December 16 decided to send to London his trusted Gustav Löwenhielm to implore British sympathy for his Danish policy, to protest the subsidy reduction, and to expose Metternich's perfidious machinations to exclude Sweden, Spain and Portugal from the peace negotiations. Alexander, Bernadotte wrote, would surely denounce this duplicity; the Prince *"nieroit l'existence du soleil dans un beau jour d'été plutôt que de douter d'Alexandre."* Through Thornton at the same time Bernadotte warned Castlereagh that the continental powers wished to exclude British goods from the continent. But Castlereagh had departed, and Löwenhielm could not gage what impression he made upon Liverpool's "dignity, aplomb, and calm."[45]

The end of December, 1813, was indeed the worst time to defend Sweden's policy in London. Just before he started for the continent, on the twenty-seventh, Castlereagh complained bitterly to Rehausen that Carl Johan had broken three promises to send his main

[45] G. Löwenhielm's notes and instructions, Dec. 16-19, 1813, SRA G. L. Sam; G. Löwenhielm to Carl Johan, Jan. 11, 14, 1814, SRA; Webster, *Castlereagh*, 514-515; Rehausen's despatches, SRA, Napoleon 11, and Anglica.

force to Holland, and that the Holstein move was unnecessary. Why, he asked, was Sweden not satisfied with Trondhjem and the other indemnities, terms to which Austria had brought Denmark? He threatened to end Swedish "tergiversation" by stopping the subsidy. Britain's interest in Holland and accumulated misinformation had seemingly been used to the full by the clever Pozzo di Borgo.[46]

In the lair of the sovereigns at Frankfort one group of military men wished to get rid of Bernadotte at any cost. Another group was less hostile. The Prussians had ceased to say much, for they hoped to acquire some of the Swedish conquests. Nesselrode considered the winter lull an excellent moment for the Danish campaign, and the Tsar made convincing assurances. Metternich, however, appeared as the personification of the evil one. He was chagrined and surprised at the failure of Bombelles.[47] He still hoped for some compromise settlement between Sweden and Denmark and on December 24 suggested four methods to Alexander.

I. Trondhjem and the fort of Fredrikshald to Sweden at once, with further arrangements at the peace; Swedish evacuation of Holstein; Danish coöperation with the allies.

[46] Rehausen to Carl Johan, Dec. 27, 1813 (copy in Rehausen to Engeström, Dec. 28), SRA, Anglica. The missing original may have been destroyed by Wetterstedt in order not to disturb the Crown Prince's mind during the Kiel negotiations, when it reached headquarters.

[47] *Castlereagh Corr.*, IX, 109-110, 126; Löwenhielm to Wetterstedt, Dec. 19, 25, 30, 1813, Jan. 2, 1814, SRA; A. Fournier, *Der Congress von Chatillon* (Vienna, Prague, 1900), 359, 360; Pertz, *Stein*, III, 503; Weil, *Mémoires du Général-Major Russe Baron de Löwenstern* (2 vols., Paris, 1903), II, 237ff.

II. Trondhjem and the two forts at once; the rest of Norway to Sweden at the peace; evacuation of Holstein; Danish coöperation with the allies; Swedish Pomerania to be distributed with other indemnities at the general peace.

III. Same as II without Danish coöperation.

IV. Cession of Norway and counter-cession of Pomerania "admitted in principle," the two forts to Sweden at once, and evacuation of Holstein; peace between Denmark and the allies through Austrian mediation and on liberal terms.[48]

Alexander thought none of these sufficient, so proposed: immediate cession of Trondhjem and Fredrikshald; Sweden's retention of Holstein until receipt of all Norway; placing both Pomerania and Guadeloupe among the general indemnities; Danish coöperation or not as she wished. In return for this proposal which he claimed to be a triumph over Metternich the Tsar asked Bernadotte to hasten to France with his army and held out high hopes for what Providence had in store for him.[49]

Metternich, beaten, threw up the game. On December 31 he renounced his rôle of mediator, and with shame and regret asked Bombelles to tell Rosenkrantz that Austria was forced by the allies to stand against her own principles; Sweden's claims now being what force alone could impose, no mediator could be useful. Privately Metternich blazed forth his anger: let Berna-

[48] Nielsen, *Akt. Bidrag . . . 1813 og 1814*, 81-83; Schinkel, *Minnen, Bihang*, III, 240.

[49] Löwenhielm to Carl Johan, Dec. 24, 30, 1813, SRA; Schinkel, *Minnen*, VIII, 369.

dotte abandon the alliance and retire to his northern rocks.[50]

Austria's angry withdrawal left Bernadotte free to settle the Danish affair, but with ample injunctions to settle it quickly. The invasion of Denmark became a promenade. With the fall of Glückstadt the Prince boasted that the Swedes had now done what Tilly had failed to do and what Torstenson had not dared attempt.

Denmark, with the enemy overrunning Jutland, her finances deplorable, with no hope left in France or in Austria, heard that stringent terms were on the way from Frankfort. Bourke returned with an uncompromising demand from Bernadotte and the announcement of resumption of war. At last King Frederick drank the cup of humiliation. On January 7 for the third time Bourke went to Kiel. Denmark now asked for a quick peace, agreed to cede Norway and join the allies if the Swedes would evacuate Danish territory at once, cede to Denmark Swedish Pomerania and Rügen, and help Denmark get further indemnities.[51] The Prince accepted the basis and ceased active warfare during the negotiations (January 10-14, 1814).

Honors in warfare had gone to the Swedes, but honors in the negotiations were to go to the Danish plenipotentiary, Edmond Bourke. Although Greenland, Iceland and the Faroes had always been Norwegian possessions, and Wetterstedt (Swedish pleni-

[50] Metternich to Bombelles, Dec. 31, 1813 (copy), DRA, K.A. 1813-1814; Woynar, 171-175; Metternich's private letter to Vincent (draft), Dec. 31, Vienna SA; Fournier, *Chatillon*, 44, 248.

[51] O. Alin, *Den Svensk-Norska Unionen* (Stockholm, 1889), *Bilagor*, 8-9.

potentiary) should have known it, Bourke represented it otherwise, and got definite ownership for Denmark. Danish pride and possibly a desire to avoid a contractual bond, forbade acceptance of the 1,000,000 riksdalers Sweden offered for immediate possession of Norway so Bourke persuaded the Swedes to pay this sum as a subsidy to Danish troops. Swedish Pomerania, with Rügen, was to go to Denmark as soon as Sweden held possession of Norway; elaborate safeguards for the transferred population were specified. On Bourke's insistence the King of Sweden had to be responsible for the Norwegian share of Denmark's public debt, the amount to be proportioned by a commission according to population and resources.[52]

Only after long discussions with Bernadotte did Wetterstedt agree to this latter demand, and on condition that the King was obligated only in his capacity of King of Norway. Such phraseology was not only innate Scandinavian caution. The Swedes had heard rumors that Christian Frederick might proclaim himself King of an independent Norway, and perhaps they suspected King Frederick's mental reservations. They asked Britain to continue the blockade of Norway, and Carl Johan wished to retain Holstein as a pledge. That he soon agreed to evacuate it is a tribute to the power of Bourke's assurances. Bourke had done an unpleasant task uncommonly well. In the night of January 14-15 the treaty was definitely signed.

[52] The treaty is accessible in *British and Foreign State Papers*, I, 194ff and in Martens, I, 666ff. Wetterstedt's accounts of the negotiations, and the successive treaty drafts are in SRA, Freden i Kiel; Bourke's tale is printed in Friis, 107-110. See Forssell, *Wetterstedt*, 249-254; O. Varenius, "Kieltraktaten, Dess Genesis," *Historisk Tidskrift* (1932), 129-204.

The negotiators, thinking of the present rather than of the future, appeared indifferent to whether the statement of cession of Norway read to "Sweden" or to the "King of Sweden." Hence a debate of constitutional significance arose in the eighteen-nineties: did title to Norway rest in the King or in the Swedish State? The opinion of 1814 will always be a puzzle. We know only that Bernadotte had looked for a union similar to that between Scotland and England, but no one knows how well he understood the nature of that union.[53] In Denmark's simultaneous treaty with Great Britain she did not succeed in recovering her fleet, but regained all her colonies except Helgoland, and was granted subsidies.[54]

There were tense moments at the last until Bourke's name was on the Swedish-Danish treaty, for on January 14 there arrived from London the despatches containing Castlereagh's threat to withhold the subsidy unless Bernadotte rejoined the common line of action. Perhaps the messages were not completely deciphered before the signature, but probably the ministers knew their general contents. Had Wetterstedt or Thornton informed Bernadotte that the loyal British had turned thus against him it is doubtful if he would have ad-

[53] Forssell (*Wetterstedt*) argued that the Norwegian-Swedish cession was personal; O. Alin (*Den Svensk-Norska Unionen*) and in painstaking detail in his *Fjerde Artikeln af Fredstraktaten i Kiel den 14 Jan. 1814* [Stockholm, 1899] insisted that the treaty phrase "To the King of Sweden . . ." was only a formula and really meant the Kingdom of Sweden as such. Recently the Norwegian, Wollebaek (*Om Kielertraktaten*) has taken up the general view of Forssell, and Varenius has ably refuted his thesis ("Kieltraktaten. Dess Genesis").

[54] Martens, I, 678ff. Russia made peace with Denmark on Feb. 8; Prussia delayed until Aug. 25, for reasons that will appear.

vanced a step toward Holland.  And if Bourke had
gained an inkling of the rift he might have refused to
sign.  Circumstances had changed since Castlereagh
wrote in the heat of his misconceptions, and Wetterstedt and Thornton were wisely silent even after the
treaty was signed.[55]

The treaty was received coolly.  Britain was glad to
see Carl Johan free to go to Holland but detested the
transfer of Norway.  At allied headquarters the feeling was similar.  Danish relief was flavored with bit-
terness at the injustice of it all, and at the inefficacy
of the government's policy.  Rosenkrantz begged that
he should not have to stand alone as responsible for
the policy he had never favored.[56]  In both Norway
and Pomerania, the people resented their chattel-like
barter.  In Sweden happiness in winning Norway was
"much impaired" by the report that Carl Johan would
now go to Holland.  The allied cause was unpopular,
and few of the people would have disapproved the
Prince's return to Sweden.  Engeström was full of fears
that Norway would not recognize the treaty, urged
that Holstein be held, and upbraided Wetterstedt for
letting Bourke outsmart him of the Norwegian colonies.[57]

Norway was won—on paper.  Two years of diplomacy and war had been crowned with success.  The

[55] Rehausen to Wetterstedt, Dec. 27, 1813, Wetterstedt to Rehausen,
Jan. 15, 1814, SRA, Anglica; Castlereagh to Thornton, Dec. (27?), 1813,
London FO, Sweden 80.

[56] *Meddelelser*, IX, 28-31.

[57] C. Gordon (in Jönköping) to British Foreign Office, Jan. 28, 1814,
London FO, Holland Frontiers 16; Engeström to Carl Johan, Jan. 21,
24, SRA.

Crown Prince had been deflected again and again from his main purpose by Russian delays and intrigues, by the demands of the general war, and by Austrian duplicity. At last he had taken affairs into his own hands, and Scandinavia now had what seemed to Bernadotte her "natural frontiers." Sweden and Norway, separated from continental boundary quarrels, could pursue the paths of peaceful industry and culture. But there was still a long, hard task ahead, a task more difficult than Bernadotte imagined when he signed the Treaty of Kiel.

# VII

## THE CAMPAIGN IN FRANCE

### To April 1814

WITH his great goal won as securely as a treaty could win it, and with his army intact, Bernadotte was free after the treaty of Kiel once more to fight for the common cause.

The "common cause" had gradually come to mean the invasion of France and the destruction of Napoleon. Bernadotte doubtless sensed the trend of events in November, 1813, and he was doubtless happy to have a task which made it impossible for him to invade France. Nevertheless, he did not invent the Danish campaign in order to avoid a French campaign. It was to acquire Norway that he had built his alliances and brought an army to the continent. Already he had been dragged farther into Germany than his judgment approved. The Swedes remembered the risks Gustavus Adolphus had taken, and that Charles XII had been caught too far from home. Napoleon had made the same mistake at Moscow. Bernadotte was too cautious to put his neck deliberately into a noose. But, by January, 1814 he had both destroyed the hostile power in his rear and assured himself of his conquest.[1] Now he had to face squarely the question of invasion of France.

Bernadotte's distaste for an invasion of his fatherland was as natural as it was obvious. When the campaign started the idea of invasion was but a vague and distant possibility; he did not have to consider it. He could, of course, hope that Napoleon might be overthrown and he be called to head a reorganized government, but that was a mere dream. When, after Leipzig, the allies pushed on toward France the former marshal earnestly denounced their plan of campaign, urged that Germany first be reorganized and stressed the dangers of a premature invasion. France must be guaranteed her "natural frontiers," he said, and taught that Napoleon was a tyrant. Otherwise the whole people would rise *en masse* and hurl the allies from France as they had done in 1794.[2] Bernadotte's argument was powerful and was backed by knowledge of the French people and by military experience, but the allies chose the venturesome way.

By the end of November Carl Johan himself was thinking of a campaign in France, though his Danish war had just begun. He procured Cassini's and Ferrari's maps of France, and convinced the Prussian Kalkreuth of his desire to pass the Rhine, where he felt sure a remarkable rôle awaited him. He urged that no armistice be granted Napoleon even if a peace

---

[1] Wellington agreed with Sir Charles Stewart that Bernadotte could not wisely leave the Danes and Davoust behind him (see *Castlereagh Corr.*, IX, 276ff).

[2] Schinkel, *Minnen*, IX, 424-429; Military Observations of Nov. 15, SRA, Högkv. Kon.; Carl Johan to Blücher, Nov. 14, BFA.

congress met.[3]  Once when he received news from Paris
he became pensive and reserved; he wanted a quick
peace with Denmark so that he could "go to conquer
peace on the Rhine and if necessary on the Seine"; he
thought "a goal nobler, greater, more worthy of the
courage" of his troops called them on.[4]  Count Selviac
de Viel-Castel came to headquarters and fired Bernadotte's ambitions anew with thoughts of kingship in
France.  Bernadotte approached King Frederick William (of all people) for his blessing on this high ambi-
tion.[5]  No wonder the allied representatives at headquarters soon thought that the Prince was *"sehr heis"*
to move on to France.  However, no matter what were
his dreams at night the campaign against Denmark
went forward by day.

While Bernadotte talked and speculated, and the
allies urged him to hurry, voices were raised against
his further march to the west.  After the treaty of
Kiel the Swedish people, only moderately happy at the
conquest of Norway, wished for Prince and army to
come home.[6]  The squeamish Engeström pled that the
army go no farther until Norway was actually in Swedish possession.  Tarrach suspected that the Swedes
exaggerated the rebellious attitude of Norway to serve

[3] Schulzenheim to Wetterstedt, Dec. 4, 1813, SRA, Wetterstedt's S.B.
A contributory reason for this was that Bernadotte feared to see a general
armistice tie his own hands in Denmark.

[4] Instructions to Tawast, Dec. 17, 1813 (Apostille), SRA, Högkv. Kon.;
*Meddelelser*, IX, 18.

[5] Kalkreuth to Frederick William, Nov. 22, 1813, Upsala, Alin Samling XII.

[6] See especially the British spy reports from C. Gordon, Jan. 28, 1814,
London FO, Holland Frontiers 16.

as an excuse for withdrawal from the war.[7] Metternich frankly opposed a Swedish advance. He had long feared the coöperation of Alexander and Bernadotte, far more when he learned of the plan to put the Prince on the throne of France. Under the sting of his diplomatic defeat in the Bombelles affair he condemned Swedish policy, and said Carl Johan should either coöperate or, "supposing that sincere coöperation was not to be expected," he should go enjoy his conquests and abandon the war against France; Bernadotte was a composite of *"astuce et d'arrières pensées . . . Il ne vise pas moins à se ménager—un grand rôle en France, qu'à affermir, à defaut de mieux, son existence en Suède."*[8]

Bernadotte's real feeling about a campaign in France is difficult to understand because although he was repelled by the idea of war in his homeland he was also drawn by hope of glory therein. Throughout the campaign of 1813 he did what he could to relieve the condition of French prisoners, sent them money, and often released them after delivering a lecture on the wrongdoings of their Emperor. After Dennewitz when some Swedish soldiers helped some wounded Frenchmen he exclaimed impulsively to Thornton,

"C'est inconcevable, que la tendresse avec la quelle le soldat Suédois soigne les prisonniers Français! Quel instinct!"[9]

---

[7] Stroganov to Romanzov, Dec. 15/27, 1813, Jan. 13/25, 1814, Moscow films in SRA; Tarrach to Frederick William, Dec. 31, 1813, Berlin SA, Schweden I, 15a; Feb. 22, Apr. 5, 26, 1814, Berlin SA, Corr.; Krusemarck to Hardenberg, Mar. 21, 1814 (intercepted), Paris AN, 1668; Engeström to Carl Johan, Jan. 21, 24, 1814, SRA.

[8] Metternich to Vincent, Dec. 31, 1813 (ciphered, draft #2), Vienna SA.

[9] *Castlereagh Corr.*, IX, 54; cf. *ibid.*, 48ff.

Then he realized he had said too much! Both sentiment and policy guided his attempts to build up a friendly party in France, and to convince the people that he was fighting not the French people, but only their oppressor.

Napoleon may at first have thought that Bernadotte was only "bluffing," but he also made repeated offers to entice the ex-marshal to his side. The propositions of the spring of 1812 have been mentioned. Beginning in January, 1813, the Emperor tried anew. Through agents in Hamburg he sounded the Prince, and later sent Consul Signeul with offers and flattery: for alliance with France Sweden could have Finland and an enlarged Pomerania; Bernadotte could have command of all the imperial armies.[10] The moment for a reconciliation was ill-chosen, for the Swedish treaty with Great Britain was being signed and the government had just retaliated against French debt repudiation by repudiating its debts in French territories.[11] Again in May Napoleon extended a hand of friendship through Colonel Peyron, the Swedish commander captured in Pomerania. But by this time the Swedish army already was on the continent.[12]

That any offer could have swung Bernadotte from the allies to Napoleon is highly improbable; certainly

[10] Engeström to Löwenhielm, Jan. 5, 1813, SRA, Musc.; Bassano to d'Ohsson (Swedish chargé in Paris), Feb. 13, 1813, and d'Ohsson's despatch of Feb. 15, SRA, Gallica.

[11] Copies from the *"Bureau des fonds des amortissements,"* Upsala, Schinkel Sam. IV.

[12] "Berättelse of Peyron," on interviews of Apr. 17 and 24, 1813 with Bassano, SRA, Napoleon 8 and Danmark-Norge 1; Scaevola, 355-357 and Suremain, 286f. A copy of Peyron's letter to Carl Johan is in Wetterstedt's despatches to Engeström, SRA.

none of those made could have done so, for none of them offered Norway to Sweden.

In March Emperor and Prince each decided to justify his position publicly. Napoleon ordered collection and publication of Bernadotte's correspondence showing especially his demand for Norway. The editor, however, refused to do the job because Swedish and English versions were better, and because further publication would be more harmful than helpful to France. Later someone did the work, but the Emperor rejected it, and evidently it was never printed.[13] Simultaneously Bernadotte wrote and published a long letter to Napoleon, enumerating the Emperor's crimes against Pomerania, Swedish commerce, and Europe as a whole, and ridiculing his hypocritical talk of peace.[14]

With this Napoleon let the quarrel rest for a time, of course withholding from the French people any justification of Bernadotte. The battles of Grossbeeren and Dennewitz then fanned the flames of anger, and new fuel was added by Bernadotte's letter to Marshal Ney (Sept. 9, 1813) asking for peace, and saying that both sides had ravaged Europe enough and done nothing for humanity.[15] Napoleon, beside himself with rage, now declared France would make no peace with Sweden until Sweden relinquished her claim to Guadeloupe; he ordered the French papers filled with diatribes

[13] To Bassano, Mar. 18, 24, 1813, and an unsigned memorandum, Paris AAE, N1791.

[14] Mar. 20, 1813, Paris AAE, Suède Supplement 14. Published versions, taken from the BFA, are all dated Mar. 23; Bail, 141-151; de Garden, *Histoire Générale des traités de Paix* . . . (14 vols., Paris, -1859), XIII, 363-368; Scaevola, 671-675.

[15] BFA; *Recueil*, 102.

against the traitor "Prince of Ponte Corvo," and with accusations of his mother's insanity; he advised that the "Princess of Ponte Corvo" be removed to the country and the people excited to riot against her dwelling in Paris; and he ordered Bernadotte's public pictures destroyed and his name erased from the municipal lists.[16]

Napoleon's hate was inevitable, for Bernadotte became the rallying point for those who wished to overthrow Napoleon in the name of French patriotism and liberalism. Bernadotte emphasized repeatedly that he fought not against France but only against Napoleon, that he had to do so because of his obligations to Sweden. Madame de Staël wanted her hero to be the William the Third of France. Benjamin Constant planned with him on methods of revolutionizing France. Signeul urged that he become "Mediator" between France and Europe. Deputations came from France, and Dumouriez wrote from England, "after you have been Germany's liberator through your cleverness you shall become your fatherland's savior through your wisdom."[17]

One of the memorials to Bernadotte may be cited as typical. Written probably by Benjamin Constant it advocated issuance of a proclamation by the allies appealing to the French people and stating that peace would not be made with Napoleon. If the allies objected to this agitation against a sovereign a prelimi-

[16] Napoleon to Bassano, July 15, 1813, Paris AAE, N1791; Napoleon to Minister of Police, Sept. (?), 1813 (from Dresden), Paris AN, 1700; Angeberg, Le Congrés de Vienne, 5; Lecestre, Lettres, II, 305.
[17] Oct. 28, 1813, Schinkel, Minnen, IX, 477.

nary brochure should be written attacking the legitimacy of Napoleon's authority: as a foreigner without
hereditary right, and as an oppressor without title
from the popular will. France should be deluged by
tracts sent in along those underground routes used for
years by monks, émigrés and smugglers. The right of
a people to choose its own head, and to have free,
representative institutions should be emphasized.[18]

With such influences at work on his sanguine spirit
the Prince received the French adventurer, Count
Selviac de Viel-Castel. Viel-Castel assured Bernadotte
that the French people awaited him with longing, eager
for him to rule over them, and at the end of December,
1813, got the Prince to send him, Viel-Castel, on a
mission to southern France, particularly to Bernadotte's home town of Pau in Béarn. The agent seems
to have drawn his own instructions: the avowed object
of the mission was the overthrow of the throne which
had been fed by blood and occupied by a Corsican;
France was to be informed of Bernadotte's sentiments
for his country; Viel-Castel was to form a "French
Guard" (flag, motto, etc. are all described); a *Chambre
d'État* was to be established at Bordeaux with a five-
man executive of which the Crown Prince of Sweden
was to become president; he was to be also Lt.-General
of France; the *Chambre* was to choose "from among
the great men born French" a sovereign "worthy to
govern so fine an Empire"; tariffs were to be abolished,

---

[18] In November, 1813, Upsala, Alin Samling, XIII; *Castlereagh Corr.*,
IX, 117ff. Several documents have been published by the writer in *Historisk
Tidskrift* (1934), III häfte, 271-280, and in the *Journal of Modern History*,
VII (1935), 41-48.

and the constitution was to be based on heredity of
the throne, equality of laws, liberty of man, and representative government.[19]  Despite the magnificent program Viel-Castel accomplished nothing, and even his
transfer to the Bourbon cause did not save him from
ending up in a Bordeaux jail.

Bernadotte meantime forced on Denmark the treaty
of Kiel.  He then evacuated Holstein, giving up thus
the only guarantee he had for the transfer of Norway,
and took the army to Holland by rapid marches.
Winzingerode's corps (under Bernadotte's command)
had crossed the Rhine January 1, 1814, but none of
Bernadotte's command had any part in the early advance in France which led to the victory of La Rothiére
(February 1) or the later chastisement of Blücher's
too-eager army.  Bernadotte himself had hastened to
Cologne, but the first Swedish troops did not cross the
Rhine until February 24; they halted then at Liége
for weeks of exasperating inactivity.[20]  A complication
of incidents had wounded the Prince's pride and re-
awakened his suspicion and reserve; perhaps, too, he
was waiting for a sign from France.

Bernadotte had early realized that the first peace
conference, however informal, would determine the
trend of European settlement, and he therefore insisted that a Swedish representative be present.  He
struggled against the invidious distinction between
large and small powers, and felt especially that he who

[19] Scott, *Historisk Tidskrift* (1934), III-häfte, 275-277.
[20] See orders in *Recueil*.  Schulzenheim to Wetterstedt, Feb. 11, said
the Prince Royal's plan was to unite all his various corps between Rheims
and Soissons (SRA, Napoleon 12).

had helped to build the coalition should not be elbowed
out when powerful states were ready to dictate victor's
terms. He feared especially that the allies might par-
tition his beloved France.[21] Hence both his fears for
France and his intense pride were aroused when his
accredited representative (C. Löwenhielm) was refused
admission to the Congress of Châtillon.

Angrily the Prince wrote Löwenhielm: how did the
four powers presume a tutelage over Sweden, one of
the first states in the alliance? Had she done some
wrong? If Sweden had no right in preliminary con-
ferences how could she have more in the final congress?
Although Sweden had attained her special aim (and so
had each of the others) she was as much interested as
they in the general settlement; if Sweden's rights were
not recognized she had the privilege of making a separate peace. Löwenhielm should tell the three sovereigns and Castlereagh that Bernadotte awaited their
reply before he decided whether to enter France or to
retire with his army to Sweden.[22]

While Bernadotte fulminated from Cologne Wetterstedt followed the allied headquarters, as best he could,
in the irregular advance. He saw the divergent opinions of the allies, the Austrian fear of Alexander's Polish
designs and of his desire to set Bernadotte on the
throne of France, the Austrian hesitance in the war

[21] To his son Oscar, Feb. 25, 1814, BFA; Löwenhielm to Hardenberg
(and to the other Ministers), Jan. 28, 1814, Hardenberg to Löwenhielm
Feb. 11 (copy), Berlin SA, XI, 249-2; Nesselrode to Löwenhielm, Jan.
22/Feb. 3, Löwenhielm to Carl Johan, Feb. 3, SRA. See C. Dupuis, *Le
Ministère de Talleyrand* (Paris, 1919), II, 215ff.

[22] Schulzenheim to Löwenhielm, to Wetterstedt, Feb. 15, 17, 1814, SRA,
Napoleon 12. Cf. Wetterstedt to Löwenhielm, Feb. 24, SRA.

and the Russian and Prussian bloodthirsty aggressiveness. The situation undoubtedly increased the feeling of both Wetterstedt and Carl Löwenhielm that Sweden was fortunately outside the circle of these wrangles and futile wars. Löwenhielm did not want to attend the congress even if invited, and Wetterstedt could not understand why Sweden should meddle in continental affairs.[23] Only Carl Johan and the eagle-eyed Engeström from his distant perch felt the exclusion as a blow to Swedish prestige, and sensed permanent danger in the great-power *versus* small-power distinction. Wetterstedt mentioned the matter "very mildly" to Alexander and was satisfied with the explanation that a negotiating group must be kept small; on the question of the new-forming alliance he had nothing to say to Castlereagh or to advise his Prince. The Swedish chancellor was likewise conciliatory about Guadeloupe, for France was adamant on its return. This moderate attitude, and Prussian desire for Pomerania, won encouragement for the suggestion that Bernadotte's son Oscar marry the younger daughter of Frederick William, and an invitation to Carl Johan to be present at the final settlement in Vienna.[24]

Wetterstedt's informative reports and their implications of an early peace made Bernadotte, far from the scene of action, tense with mingled hope and mis-

[23] Wetterstedt to Carl Johan, Feb. 9, 15, 18, 1814, SRA, Napoleon 12; Mikhailowitch, *Alexandre*, 131f; Sorel, VIII, 250; Löwenhielm to Schulzenheim, Jan. 16, 23, Löwenhielm to Carl Johan, Feb. 23, 24, 1814, to Wetterstedt, Dec. 30, SRA.

Flahaut to Minister of Police (?) (Feb. 28, Paris AN, 1669) indicates that France realized these allied differences of opinion even at the time.

[24] Wetterstedt to Carl Johan, Feb. 9 *et seq.*, 1814, SRA, Napoleon 12.

trust. With renewed insistence he demanded admission to the Congress of Châtillon, but he had already renounced the rash threat of withdrawal. Honor demanded, he said, that Sweden obtain compensation for Denmark; Prussia must be told that Pomerania had already been ceded to Denmark. Instead of a general alliance he preferred separate alliances with Russia and Great Britain. Guadeloupe should be yielded for the sake of peace, but Sweden should then obtain Surinam and Curaçao. As for France the sovereigns should be informed that they stood on a volcano: if someone should kill Napoleon, France would rise at the voice of a single courageous leader and the allied armies would be fortunate to regain the Rhine.[25]

These despatches, crossing each other en route, made it impossible for Bernadotte to achieve his ends. The allies had only to put the question to Carl Johan once more and thereby gain two weeks to do as they pleased: they recognized Sweden's "right" to be at Châtillon, but it was a question of four or twenty-four; if Sweden were admitted then Spain would have to be, and others; would not the Prince trust them?[26] Wetterstedt was informed of the progress of the baffling negotiations. He in turn had modified the Prince's orders to Löwenhielm, for he was horrified at the threats of withdrawal,

[25] Schulzenheim to Wetterstedt, Feb. 25, 28, 1814, SRA, Napoleon 12.

[26] Löwenhielm to Carl Johan, Feb. 26, Mar. 18, 1814, Wetterstedt to Carl Johan, Feb. 25 to Mar. 23 (almost daily) SRA, Napoleon 12; Schinkel, *Minnen*, VIII, 301; *Castlereagh Corr.*, IX, 292-295; Schulzenheim to Wetterstedt, Mar. 4, 10, SRA, Napoleon 12; Carl Johan to Wetterstedt, Mar. 10, SRA, Napoleon 13; to Löwenhielm, Mar. 13, BFA.

See also Webster, *Castlereagh*, 193-232; Fournier, *Congress*; Forssell, *Wetterstedt*, 278ff, 311-356, *passim*; Krusemarck to Frederick William, Feb. 21, 1814, Berlin SA, Krus.

threats which were "ridiculous and harmful to Swedish interest," and he correctly surmised that they would be revoked when Gascon anger gave way to Béarnais caution.[27] Nevertheless the Prince was not moved by the allies' appeals, and he was irritated with Wetterstedt's indifference; his intense interest in the settlement with France and the pride of a parvenu both required him to have his finger on the pulse of events. He ordered Löwenhielm to proceed at once to Châtillon and Wetterstedt to return to his headquarters at Liége. But Wetterstedt delayed the execution even of these positive commands because when he received them, March 10, the Congress was awaiting a French reply to its ultimatum and might disband; before Löwenhielm reached Châtillon there was no congress. Against the indifference of his ministers and the strategy of the four-power-men Carl Johan's insistence had been powerless.

When Castlereagh at last obtained the long-sought permanent alliance by the treaty of Chaumont (March 10, 1814) Wetterstedt was asked what Swedish intentions were as to accession. The Chancellor had powers only to take the question *ad referendum*, but no time to refer; he therefore told Castlereagh that Sweden considered the obligations of such an alliance too burdensome. Certainly Sweden could hardly agree to put 60,000 men into the field in case of a new threat from France. The matter was dropped.[28] Once more the

[27] Wetterstedt to Löwenhielm, Feb. 24, 1814 (private), Stockholm KB, Wetterstedt Samling; Wetterstedt to Carl Johan, Feb. 24, Schulzenheim to Wetterstedt, Feb. 18, SRA, Napoleon 12.

[28] Wetterstedt to Carl Johan, Mar. 10, 13, 1814, SRA, Napoleon 12; Löwenhielm to Carl Johan, Mar. 26, SRA. Carl Johan had already told

great powers, Great Britain, Russia, Austria and Prussia had acted successfully as a separate and continuing group.

Before these questions of peace negotiations and general alliances had been settled by time a new source of irritation had arisen. Blücher's rash aggressiveness had cost him defeats and heavy losses. He needed reinforcements. Three of Bernadotte's corps (under Winzingerode, Bülow, and Woronzov) had entered France and were close to Blücher, but the logical step of attaching these corps to Blücher was feared because of Bernadotte's sensitiveness.

Castlereagh promised to appease the Prince. He had the British force of General Graham in the Netherlands put under Bernadotte's orders, and suggested naming Bernadotte "Generalissimo" in the north. The soothing oil of flattery was poured thickly: Bernadotte's warnings against a premature invasion of France were proving only too true, he was told; this was why Blücher needed new troops. Bernadotte could best guide future operations; would he advise immediate concentration in central France, or a preliminary thorough conquest of the Low Countries? Should not Antwerp be captured? Britain valued it infinitely. Out of delicacy for Bernadotte's sentiments the allies suggested he campaign in the Netherlands instead of in France.[29] Two days later Castlereagh asked if

Thornton that Sweden would have too few interests in the alliance to be worth the responsibility (Thornton to Castlereagh, Feb. 17 (#15), London FO, Sweden 90).

[29] Wetterstedt to Carl Johan, Feb. 26, 1814, SRA, Napoleon 12. Cf. *Castlereagh Corr.*, IX, 292; Webster, *Castlereagh*, 221.

Bernadotte could come to a new conference like the Trachenberg meeting.[30]  Count Ozarovsky came from the Tsar to present in the best light possible the withdrawal of the advanced corps.[31]  All was done with the utmost tact and with beautiful phraseology, though even Bernadotte must have realized that impatience with his slowness and distrust of his policy were the real reasons for taking his troops.

Bernadotte had to admit the allies' right to detach his corps temporarily while he remained distant, and he took a cautious attitude.  But when he perceived that the change of command was to be permanent he protested that his army was taken from him just as he was ready to act.  He sent word to the Tsar and his colleagues that he would advance as soon as his army was returned to him.  At the same moment he urged peace with the French, thereby making the allies less willing to entrust their troops to him—which may have been exactly what he wanted.[32]

Troubles did not end for Bernadotte even with these grievances against his allies.  Engeström had long been warning the Prince against Danish-Norwegian perfidy, and urgently advised that Holstein be held as a pledge.

[30] Wetterstedt to Carl Johan, Feb. 28, 1814, SRA, Napoleon 12.

[31] Alexander to Carl Johan, Feb. 14/26, 1814, SRA, Främ. Suv.; Schinkel, *Minnen*, VIII, 301-303; Forssell, *Wetterstedt*, 335-336.

[32] Thornton to Castlereagh, Mar. 4, 1814, London FO, Sweden 90; Krusemarck to Frederick William, Feb. 21, 1814, Berlin SA, Krus.; Krusemarck to Frederick William, Mar. 5, Alin Samling XII; Carl Johan to Duke of Saxe-Weimar, Mar. 5, etc., BFA; Schulzenheim to Wetterstedt, Mar. 10, SRA, Napoleon 12; Tingsten, *Huvuddragen . . . 1814* (Stockholm, 1925), 73f; A. Alison, *Lives of Lord Castlereagh and Sir Charles Stewart . . .* (2 vols., Edinburgh, 1861), II, 316ff.  The French learned about this affair through the interception of a despatch from Krusemarck (Mar. 17, Paris AN, 1668).

Now it appeared that the foreign minister's worst fears were to materialize. Early in March Carl Johan received from General Essen news that Christian Frederick had made himself regent of Norway and had begun to issue paper money, and that the Norwegian people were girding themselves for war to nullify the agreement made at Kiel. Immediately the allies were asked to support Sweden against possible rebellion in Norway, and they agreed to postpone ratification of their treaties with Denmark, and to maintain the blockade of Norway. But the cloudy skies to the north made Bernadotte still more hesitant to venture into France, and far more eager for peace.[33]

The Gascon Prince stood at the border of his native land at the head of a foreign army. Yet he lacked both the will and the power to act decisively, part of his army was detached, his subsidies were diminished, his advice was disregarded. Excluded from the councils of the coalition he now saw not only that Norway might slip from his grasp, but feared that his beloved fatherland might be partitioned by his own victory-intoxicated allies. The sheer discomfort of his position is hard to parallel. He stood at the Rubicon, restrained by anxiety for Norway and his position in Sweden, beckoned on by the prospect of the fair throne of France.

In the helplessness and ignorance of his isolation he eagerly read the reports of his agents in Paris. To the

French officers who came into his power he appealed for peace and sent them into France to spread the news of his greatness and his magnanimity.[34] He heard Benjamin Constant's appeals to save France from Napoleon and from the allies, and proclaimed that France must be maintained but forced to recognize the independence of other states.[35] To Dr. Franzenberg, sent by Joseph Bonaparte, he said Napoleon must make peace. To M. Chabannes, who came to him from the Bourbons, he gave the impression that he would support Louis XVIII. To Thornton, he promised he would fight the Emperor in the heart of France if he refused terms. His only consistent policy was peace, which he urged on both Napoleon and Alexander, while he hoped that out of the welter of circumstance he might himself be called to a high destiny in France.[36]

In order to gain peace on the continent and allied support in Norway Bernadotte took three important steps during March, each without waiting for the result of the previous one. First he ordered Wetterstedt to demand the return of the Russian and Prussian auxiliaries and to insist on peace: "a war in France conflicts with the interests of Europe and especially of Sweden; a war to reëstablish another dynasty is a war unjust in its bases,

[34] Rovigo to Napoleon, Feb. 23, 24, 1814, Report to Rovigo from Cologne, Mar. 11, Paris AN, 1043; Webster, *British Diplomacy*, 134; Vincent to Metternich, Feb. 21, Vienna SA.

[35] Feb. 12, 1814, *Recueil*, 639-640.

[36] This phase of the subject I have treated in more detail in "Bernadotte and the Throne of France, 1814," *Journal of Modern History*, V (1933), 165-178. See also E. J. Knapton, "Some Aspects of the Bourbon Restoration of 1814," *Journal of Modern History*, VI (1934), 405-424.

barbaric through the misfortunes it brings." Sweden should not sacrifice her children for such a war; only against France's ruler was there just complaint. "Let us have the courage to say: no war if it must be continued in opposition to the bases on which we took up arms."[37]

The second step began with a council of war at Liége in which it was agreed unanimously that France should not be deprived of her "natural boundaries," and that the Swedes should withdraw if the allies fought on for the boundaries of 1792. Ten questions were to be asked the allies—on the Châtillon negotiations, the Netherlands, the Bourbons, and the return of Bernadotte's auxiliaries. General Skjöldebrand went with these questions to the allies, charged also to get them to declare Christian Frederick a rebel and incapable of inheriting the throne of Denmark, and to ask if Sweden might withdraw her troops to Norway if imperious necessity required. But Skjöldebrand and his despatches were captured and taken before Napoleon. Now the general had to listen to an impressive harangue by the Emperor to the effect that no one had done him so much damage as the marshal whom he had permitted to become Crown Prince of Sweden; would Bernadotte now devastate his own fair France? "Tell the Crown Prince to remember that he is born a Frenchman."[38]

[37] Carl Johan to Wetterstedt, Mar. 13, 1814, BFA; Maison to Neufchatel, Feb. 27, Paris AN, 1667.

[38] Schinkel, *Minnen*, VIII, 332-333; Skjöldebrand's instructions, Mar. 17, 1814, Upsala, Alin Samling XIII; Alin, *Unionen, Bilagor*, 91-92; Skjöldebrand to Carl Johan, Apr. 15, 1814, Upsala, Schinkel Samling VI. See also Skjöldebrand's account written at Carl Johan's request in 1821: *Memoarer*, V, 155-169.

This abortive mission and the idea of Swedish retirement brought on the Prince a stern reproof from Wetterstedt. How dared Sweden, asked the Chancellor, detach herself from the coalition and openly condemn Britain's favorite project of conquering Belgium and the left bank of the Rhine? Might not Sweden need British support in Norway? Would Europe gain peace by Sweden's supporting Napoleon's demands? And how could one deal with Napoleon except by destroying him—that is, by war? The allies would neither hinder nor aid the return of the Bourbons. The Prince had said his treaties neither required nor considered the passage of the Rhine; true, said Wetterstedt, but they said all would make war and peace together, and the Rhine was not mentioned as a limit. Why did Carl Johan need auxiliaries if he was to stay in the Netherlands? Wetterstedt's able argument closed with an appeal to the Prince not to allow a sentiment honorable to France but dangerous for Sweden to jeopardize the prize he had won.[39]

But while Wetterstedt's bold objections were on the road the third step was being taken. On March 22 more disturbing news arrived from Norway and Bernadotte told Thornton he would like to go to main headquarters; two days later, after receipt of news from Paris, he determined to go at once. Early on the twenty-fifth he started, incognito, with Thornton following twenty-four hours behind. His ideas are fortunately preserved in a memorandum of March 22.

[39] Mar. 22, 1814, *Handlingar ur Brinkmanska Arkivet*, II, 230-234. See also Forssell, *Wetterstedt*, 352-355 and 342-344; Wetterstedt to Carl Johan, Mar. 15, SRA, C. J. Papper 69-3.

According to this memorandum there was no hope for France while "the tyrant" remained; if Bernadotte had not seemed to contribute with all his power to the tyrant's overthrow it was because he wanted to know the will of the people before he acted; if worthy and patriotic representatives of the nation would let him know their will he would act to repress Jacobinism and to establish constitutional authority; he would be guided by no private interests but only by concern for the welfare of France.[40]

With such a platform Bernadotte started on his trip to headquarters. Perhaps he expected to find in session the proposed meeting of French deputies, and to be hailed with enthusiasm as the man of the hour. Instead he discovered when he reached Nancy that Skjöldebrand had been captured, and that it was impossible to reach the sovereigns. He found also that the reëstablishment of the Bourbons was almost accomplished—without his aid. He wanted to be at least a "mediator," but no mediator was needed, and he was not where he could "mediate." He refused to call on Monsieur (later Charles X) pleading his incognito and the possible feeling of the Swedes. His first reaction was to attempt again to reach headquarters by circling around through Namur, but he gave that up and hurried back to Liége. On the way he met the Count Bouillé, with an offer to him to be Generalissimo of France for the Bourbons. It was not enough. With expressions of personal attachment and references to his problem in Norway he rejected the

[40] Scott, *Historisk Tidskrift* (1934), 279-280.

offer.  When he reached Liége he heard of the allied entry into Paris.

The Napoleonic drama had reached its climax.  It had raced to conclusion with a speed which astonished Bernadotte and left him helpless.  Frantically he planned to sweep into France with his army, swelling his forces with volunteers on the road to Paris.  Then his sanguine hopes were dashed by the cold after-dose of realization: France, under the expert guidance of Talleyrand, had turned to the despised Bourbons, and even Alexander had dropped his friend Bernadotte. Fate had to be accepted.  Now that the temporarily glittering prospects of a French crown had been shattered the Crown Prince of Sweden set himself to strengthen his position in the north.  Throughout the conflict his antagonism to Napoleon and his hopes in France had occupied a secondary position; now they had no position at all, and even the Hundred Days of 1815 could not stir the dying embers to life.

Unhappily he went alone to Paris in April, 1814. He was under a cloud of suspicion from his allies and he was unpopular in his native land where both then and for a century to come he was regarded as a traitor by a people who did not understand.  After two weeks in the chilly atmosphere of Paris he went north for the last time.  Braced by promises of allied aid against Norway, he was ready with renewed vigor, and a certain resignation, to build a strong Scandinavian monarchy which could resist the trend toward legitimacy and grow more popular with the passing years, the only "Napoleonic" dynasty that still survives.

# BIBLIOGRAPHY

REFERENCES herein are largely to archive material, because of the incompleteness and unreliability of the published documents. The only unexplored material which might throw light upon the subject lies, probably, in the inaccessible portions of the Bernadotte Family Archives; and even from this material Professor Oscar Alin took numerous copies which are now in the University Library at Upsala. In the section on secondary works in this bibliography there is no attempt to list the vast body of general material, but only the works particularly valuable for this study.

## UNPUBLISHED DOCUMENTS

(Abbreviations used in footnotes here in italics)
*STOCKHOLM:*
BFA—Bernadotteska Familje Arkiv
KB—Kunglig Bibliotek (Royal Library)
      Engeström Samling
      Wetterstedt Samling
SRA—Sveriges Riksarkiv
   I. Diplomatica: regular diplomatic series, including Anglica, Borussica, Danica, Gallica, Muscovitica, Turcica, and the following special series:
      Knut Bildts Depecher (*Bildt Dep.*)
      Greve Gustav Löwenhielms Brev til Carl Johan
      Hegardts Brefväxling 1812-1815 (*Hegardt Bref*)
      Högkvarterets Koncepter (*Högkv. Kon.*)
      Högkvarteret till Svenska Regeringen 1813
      Originaltraktater

Protokol i Ministeriella och Liknande Ärenden,
Supplement
Ryska Kejsarhusets Originalbrev 1797-1824
Statsrådsprotokoller 1810-1813
Utrikesstatsministers Koncepter (*U.S.K.*)
Wetterstedts Särskilda Beskickningar (*Wetterstedts
SB*)
II. Svenska Utrikesdepartmentets Dossierer Deponerad
i Riksarkivet (largely regular diplomatic material
once classified by subject, now in process of being
returned to regular locations; much of it has no rec-
ognized title).
*C. J. Papper*—Carl Johans Papper: includes—
Bref af . . . Engeström till Carl Johan 1813-1814
(6 vols.)
Depecher till Kronprinsen . . . "C.J.6, 69-3"
(*69-3*)
"C.J. 6—1814-1847. 70-4" (*70*)
1811-1813 Handlingar ur Konung Carl Johans
Papper, "C.J.4. 88-3" (*88*)
Schinkel, Upsala Papper 1810-1814 (*101*)
*Danmark-Norge*—Fascicles cited include #1, 5, 7a, 7b,
8, 9, 10, 11, 12, 13, 14, 15, 16.
*D-1814*—Diverse, 1814
*Freden i Kiel*—#7a and 7b from Danmark-Norge,
above.
*Främ. Suv.*—Främmande Suveråners Bref till Carl
Johan
*Int. Brev*—Intercepterade Bref Franska och Norska
*Napoleon*—Kriget mot Kejsar Napoleon, #7-13, 130
*Norge*—#18, 23a, 24
*Snör*—Lösa Handlingar omslagna med ett snör
*U.D. 60-11*—(few copies of Suchtelen to Tsar, 1812)
*71-5, 95, 96*—(three folios of miscellany)
III. Särskilda Samlingar
*Essen Sam.* (H. H. von Essen Samling)
*G. L. Sam.*—Gustav Löwenhielm Samling

*Moscow Films*—(Filmed copies of Russian Archive material)

*Wirsén Sam.*—Wirsén Samling

*LUND, SWEDEN*, in University library
De la Gardie Samling: Dagbok 1813, 1814; Bilagor I-III.

*UPSALA, SWEDEN*, in University library
Alin Samling (21 folios of copies, largely from SRA and BFA)
Schinkel Samling (copies and a few originals, partly used in Schinkel's *Minnen*, and its *Bihang*)

*COPENHAGEN*
DRA—Danmarks Rigsarkiv
    I. Departmentet for udenrigs Angelegenheder
        *Bernstorff* Østrig II (52), Depecher 1813-1815
        *Blome*, Rusland II Depecher 1812-1814
        Brev fra . . . Rosenkrantz til Frederick VI 1810-1824
        *Dolgorouki*—Prinds Dolgoroukys Sendelse hertil . . . og Greve Carl Moltkes overordentlige sendelse . . .
        *Forestillinger* 1813-1814
        *Sverrig Ie* (64) Korrespondancesager . . . . 1812-1813
        *Sverrig II* Depecher 1812-1813 (131)
        *Rusland Id* Greve Carl Moltkes sendelse 1813-1815
    II. *Geh. Reg.*—Geheim Registratur
    III. *K. A. 1813-1814*—Kabinetsarkivet, 1808-1889, Diverse Sager
    IV. Privatarkiv
        Blome Privat Arkiv
        Kaas Privat Arkiv

*BERLIN*
Berlin SA—Preussische Geheimstaatsarchiv:
    *Schweden I, 15a*—Rep. I Schweden No. 15a, fol. 110.
    Correspondance particulière avec M le B[on] Tarrach.

*I, 20*—AAI, Schweden, Rep. I, No. 20.
Acta Secreta . . . 1812-1813.
*Suède I, 23*—AAI, Suède Rep. I No. 23.
Depêches du et au Sr. de Tarrach 1813.
*Suède I, 24*—AAI, Suède Rep. I No. 24.
Gesandschafts Berichte von Stockholm 1813-1814.
*Corr.*—AAI, Suède Rep. I No. 25, 26.
Stockholm Correspondance avec le mission du Roi.
*Nor.*—Rep. XI, 249, a.3. fasc. 200.
Affaires relatives à la cession de la Norvège 1814.
*XI, 249*—Rep. XI, 249, a.3. fasc. 201.  Schweden.
Die Vereinigung Norwegens mit Schweden 1814.
*XI, 249-2*—Rep. XI, 249. a.3. fasc. 201. Schweden.
Schwedens Antheil an den Friedensverhandlungen 1814.
*K.P. S.*—Rep. 92 Hardenberg G 2.
Acta betr. des Kronprins von Schweden Reisen, . . .
    1813.
*Krus.*—Rep. 92 Hardenberg G 4, folio 75.
Die Sendung des Gen. v. Krusemarck . . . 1814.
*Bülow*—
Acta betr. das dem K. von Schweden H. Q. . . . 1813-
    1814.
*Dan.*—AAI, Rep. VI, Wiener Congress, Litt. D. No. 4.
Acta betr. die Angelegenheiten Dänemarcks 1814-1815.

*VIENNA*
*Vienna SA*—Haus-, Hof-, und Staatsarchiv
    Intercepte: 1812, vol. VII, VIII; 1813, vol. IX, X.
    Drucke und copia.
    Suède, 1813-1815.
        Neipperg an Metternich, Jan. 1813-May 1813.
        K. Franz I an Kronprinz v. Schweden, Aug. 20, 1813-
        Mar. 20, 1814.
        Correspondance de S.M.l'Empereur Alexandre avec le
        Prince Royal de Suède
        Kronprinz von Schweden an K. Franz I, May 23, 1813-
        Nov. 5, 1814.
        Metternich an Bildt (Nov.-Dec. 6, 1814)

Weisungen an Vincent (Sept. 13, 1813-Apr. 6, 1814).
Metternich an Neipperg (Jan. 16, 1813-Apr. 8, 1813).
Vincent an Metternich:
    #1. Jan.-Mar. 1814
    #2. Sept. 5-Oct. 30, 1813.
Weiss an Metternich (May 25-Dec. 28, 1813).
Wetterstedt (Aug. 14, 1813-May 7, 1814).
Binder an Metternich 1813, #1; Jan. 5-July 12, 1813, #2.
Engeström an Neipperg (Feb. 12-Apr. 20, 1813).
Note der Schwedische Regierung (undated 1813).
Varia (Nothing important).
Varia-Truchsacher
Undatierte 1813.

## PARIS

  *Paris AAE*—Archives des Affaires Étrangères
    *S298*—Correspondance Politique: Suède 298, Rumigny
      1813-1814
    *S. Supp. 14*—Corr. Pol.: Suède, 1795-1813, Supple-
      ment 14
    *D187*—Corr. Pol.: Danemarc 1813-1815, #187, 188, 189
    Lettres et Ordres de Napoléon, Nos. 1790-1794
      (*N1790, N1791, N1792, N1794*)
  *Paris AN*—Archives Nationales, series "AF-IV"
    *203*—Registre de Correspondance pour la Régence au
      1813
    *1041*—Correspondance de l'Archichanceller 1814
    *1043*—Correspondance du Ministère de la Police, 1814
    *1099*—Guerre, Extracts de la Corr. du Ministre, 1813-
      1814
    *1100*—Guerre, Lettres au Ministre
    *1667*—Guerre, Campagne de France, Corr. du Major-
      Gen.
    *1668*—Guerre, Campagne de France, Police de l'Armée
    *1669*—Guerre, Campagne de France, Lusigny Negotia-
      tions, etc.
    *1670*—Guerre, Campagne de France, Corr. des Maré-
      chals

*1700*—(Bernadotte to Napoleon, etc.)

*LONDON*

*London FO*—Public Record Office MSS, Foreign Office
(For several of these categories the material used is
from notes of Prof. C. K. Webster's)
*Sweden*, folios #71-90
*Prussia*, folios #86-91
*Great Britain*, folios #24, 25
*Russia*, folio #87; *Supplement, Russia*, folio #343
*Continent*, folio #4
*Frontiers of Holland*, folio #16

## PUBLISHED DOCUMENTS

Alin, Oscar, *Den Svensk-Norska Unionen. Bilagor.* Stockholm, 1889.

d'Angeberg, Comte (J. L. B. Chodzko), *Le Congrès de Vienne
et les Traités de 1815.* 2 vols., Paris, 1864.

Anker, C. J., *Utdrag ur Danska Diplomaters meddelanden
från Stockholm 1807-1808, 1810 och 1812-1813.* Translated by F. U. Wrangel. Stockholm, 1897. (Cited as
Anker-Wrangel).

Bail, M., *Correspondance de Bernadotte . . . avec Napoléon
. . . 1810-1814.* Paris, 1819.

*Bathurst MSS*, (publ. by Historical Manuscripts Commission
of Great Britain): *Report on the Manuscripts of Earl
Bathurst preserved at Cirencester Park.* London, 1923.

Boëthius, S. J. (ed.), *Bihang, Minnen ur Sveriges Nyare
Historia . . . af B. von Schinkel.* 3 vols., Upsala, 1881-
1883.

*British and Foreign State Papers, 1812-1814*, vol. I, London,
1841.

Castlereagh (See Vane).

Clercq, Alexander (ed.), *Recueil des Traités de la France,
publié sous les auspices du Ministère des affaires étrangères.*
Vol. 24. Paris, 1880.

Colenbrander, Herman Theodoor, *Gedenkstukken der Alge-meene Geschiedenis van Nederland van 1791 tot 1840. Riids Geschiedenis.* 7 *Deel, 1813-1815.* Hague, 1914.

*Correspondance inédite de l'empereur Alexandre et de Berna-dotte pendant L'année 1812 publiée par X.* Paris, 1909. Dependable, despite the invective against Bernadotte in the introduction.

*Correspondance de Napoléon I$^{er}$.* 32 vols., Paris, 1858-1870.

Fournier, August, *Gentz und Wessenberg. Briefe des Erste an den Zweiten.* Vienna and Leipzig, 1907.

Friis, Aage, *Nye Aktstykker vedrørende de Politiske Forhand-linger i Kjøbenhavn i December 1813 og Kielerfreden i Januar 1814.* Copenhagen, 1898. Reprint from *Danske Magazin,* 5 Raekke, 4 Bd.

Garden, Comte de, *Histoire Générale des Traités de Paix.* . . . 14 vols., Paris, -1859.

*Gentz und Wessenberg Briefe* (See Fournier).

Holm, Edvard, "Nogle Akstykker til Danmarks Udenrigs-politik i 1813," *Danske Magazin,* VI R., II B (1914), 61-70.

Kaas, Frederik Julius, *Frederik den Sjettes Udsoning med Napoleon. Breve fra Kancellipräsident Kaas under hans Sendelse til det Franske Hovedkvarter i Mai og Juni 1813.* Udgivet af Generalstaben. Copenhagen, 1894.

Lecestre, Léon, *Lettres Inédites de Napoléon I$^{er}$.* Vol. II, 1810-1815. (2$^{nd}$ ed.) 1897.

de Martens, F., *Recueil des Traités et conventions conclus par la Russie.* . . . 15 vols., St. Petersburg, 1874-1909.

de Martens, George Frederic, *Nouveau Recueil de Traités Supplément au Recueil des Princepaux Traités.* . . . Tome V: 1808-1814. Göttingen, 1817.

*Meddelelser fra Krigsarkiverne.* Udgivne af Generalstaben, 9 vols., Copenhagen, 1893-1902. A rich source on Danish policy.

Nielsen, Yngvar, *Aktmaessige Bidrag til de Nordiske Rigers politiske Histoirie i 1813-og 1814.* Christiania Videnska-belig Selkskabs Forhandlingar, #12, 1877, Christiania, 1877.

Nielsen, Yngvar, *Aktmaessige Bidrag til Sveriges politiske Historie 1812-1813.* Christiania, 1876. Typical of Nielsen's earlier work; extracts from documents strung together in text form.

Nielsen, Yngvar, *Bidrag til Norges og Sveriges Historie 1812-1816*. Christiania, 1869.

Nielsen, Yngvar, *Breve fra Grev H. H. v. Essen til Kronprins Carl Johan*. Christiania, 1867.

Nielsen, Yngvar, *Indberetninger fra de østerrigske Gesandter i Kjøbenhavn 1807-1812*. Christiania, 1882.

Nielsen, Yngvar, *Kielerfreden*, Christiania, 1886.

Pflugk-Harttung, Julius von, *Das Brefreiungsjahr 1813 aus dem Akten des Geheimes Staatsarchivs*. Berlin, 1913.

*Rapport à Sa Majèsté le Roi de Suède, par Son Ministre d'État et des Affaires Étrangères, en date de Stockholm le 7 janvier 1813*. Stockholm, 1813.

*Recueil des Ordres de Mouvement, Proclamations et Bulletins de S.A.R. Le Prince de Suède, commandant en chef l'Armée combinée du Nord de L'Allemagne en 1813 et 1814*. Stockholm, 1839.

"Scaevola" [Strömbäck, K. A., ed.], *Utländska diplomaters Minnen från svenska hofvet*. Stockholm, 1885-1886.

*Sbornik imperatorskago russkago istoricheskago obshchestva* (Transactions of the Imperial Russian Historical Society), vol. XXI, XXXI, St. Petersburg, 1880, 1881. (Cited as *Sbornik*).

*Supplementary Despatches, Correspondence and Memoranda of . . . Duke of Wellington*. 15 vols., London, 1858-1872.

Vane, C. W., (Marquess of Londonderry), *Correspondence, Despatches, and other Papers, of Viscount Castlereagh*. 12 vols., London, c. 1851. (Cited as *Castlereagh Corr.*).

Webster, C. K., *British Diplomacy 1813-1815*. London 1921.

## SECONDARY WORKS
(Selected list)

Ahnfelt, Arvid, *Två Kronta Rivaler*. Stockholm, 1887.

Alin, Oscar, *Carl Johan och Sveriges yttre politik 1810-1815;* (part I, 1810-1811). Stockholm, 1899.

Alin, Oscar, *Den Svensk-Norska Unionen.* Stockholm, 1889.

Alin, Oscar, *Fjerde Artikeln af Fredstraktaten i Kiel Den 14 Jan. 1814.* Stockholm, 1899.

Alin, Oscar, *Förhandlingarna om allianstraktaten mellan Sverige och Ryssland af den 5 april/24 mars 1812.* Upsala, 1900.

Alison, Sir Archibald, *Lives of Lord Castlereagh and Sir Charles Stewart, the second and third marquesses of London-derry; with annals of contemporary events in which they bore a part.* Edinburgh, 1861.

Almquist, Helge, "Karl Johan, Utrikespolitiken och Pressen år 1813," *Scandia,* II (1929), 134ff.

Arneth, Alfred Ritter von, *Johann Friedrich von Wessenberg.* 2 vols., Vienna, 1898.

Balfour, Lady Frances (Campbell), *The Life of George, fourth earl of Aberdeen.* 2 vols., London, 1922.

Barton, Sir Dunbar Plunkett, *The Amazing Career of Berna-dotte.* London, 1929.

Bernhardi, Theodor von, *Denkwürdigkeiten aus dem leben des russ. generals Carl Friedrich, Grafen von Toll.* 4 vols. in 5, maps, etc., Leipzig, 1865-1866.

Björnstjerna, Comte de (ed.), *Mémoires Posthumes du Feld Maréchal Stedingk.* 3 vols., Paris, 1847.

Brulin, Herman, "C. A. Löwenhielm om Karl Johan," *Historisk Tidskrift* (1927), 416-439.

Buckland, C. S. B., *Metternich and the British Government from 1809 to 1813.* London, 1932.

Calmettes, Fernand, *Mémoires du Général B^on Paul Thié-bault.* 5 vols., Paris, 1895.

Clason, Sam, "Fälttågsplanen från Trachenberg," *Carl Johan Förbundets Handlingar,* (1911-1914) pp. 41-87.

Coquelle, P., "La Mission d'Alquier à Stockholm, 1810-1811," *Revue d'histoire Diplomatique,* XXIII (1909), 196-239.

Coupé de St. Donat, et de Roquefort (ed.), *Mémoires de Charles XIV Jean.* Paris, 1820.

Du Casse, Albert (ed.), *Joseph Bonaparte, Mémoires et Cor-*

*respondance politique et militaire du Roi Joseph; Publiés,
annotés et mis en ordre.* Paris, 1853-1858.

Dupuis, Charles, *Le Ministère de Talleyrand.* 2 vols., Paris,
1919.

Enander, Bo, "C. H. Anckarsvärd och 'disciplinbrottet'
1813," *Personhistorisk Tidskrift* (1931), 174-198.

Engeström, Lars von, *Minnen och Anteckningar.* Ed. by
Elof Tegnér, 2 vols., Stockholm, 1876.

Fain, Baron A. J. F., *Manuscrit de mil huit cent treize, con-
tenant le précis.* . . 2 vols., Paris, 1824.

Forssberg, Einar, *Sverige och Preussen 1810-1815.* Upsala,
1922.

Forssell, Hans L., *Minne af Statsministern Grefve Gustaf af
Wetterstedt (Svenska Akademiens Handlingar ifrån år 1886).*
Stockholm, 1889. Excellent biography.

Fournier, August, *Der Congress von Châtillon. Die politik
im kriege von 1814. Eine historische studie.* Vienna and
Prague, 1900.

Friederich, Rudolph, *Geschichte des Herbstfeldzuges 1813.* 3
vols., Berlin, 1903-1906. Best account of military affairs.

Heckscher, Eli F., *The Continental System; An Economic
Interpretation.* Oxford, 1922.

Höjer, T. T., "Carl Johans Kapitulations anbud till Davoust," *Karl Johan Förbundets Handlingar* (1931-1934),
1-29. Upsala, 1934.

Höjer, T. T., "En Hanseatisk Karl Johansbeundrare på
försommare 1813," *Historisk Tidskrift* (1934), 186-190.

Höjer, T. T., "Sverige och det tyska rekonstruktionsproblemet vintern 1812-1813," *Historisk Tidskrift* (1933), 1-81.

Holm, Edvard, *Danmark-Norges Udenrigske Historie, 1800-
1814.* 2 vols., Copenhagen, 1912.

Hormayr, Jos. (ed.), *Lebensbilder aus dem Befreiungskriege:
Ernst Friedrich Herbert Graf von Münster.* 3 vols., 1844-
1845.

Klinkowström, A. F. von Metternich-Winneburg-Oschsen-
hausen (ed.), *Oesterreichs Theilnahme an den Befreiung-
skriegen, 1813-1815.* Vienna, 1887.

Lacour-Gayet, *Talleyrand.* 2 vols., Paris, 1928-1930.

Lehman, Max, "Gneisenau's Sendung nach Schweden und England im Jahre 1812," *Historische Aufsatze und Reden,* 292-293.

Lehman, Konrad, *Die Rettung Berlins im Jahre 1813.* Berlin, 1934. New and, for a German work, astonishingly laudatory of Bernadotte.

Maude, Col. F. N., *The Leipzig Campaign 1813.* London, 1908.

Mikhailowitch, Nicholas, *L'Empereur Alexandre I$^{er}$; essai d'étude historique.* 2 vols., St. Petersburg, 1912.

Morén, F. W., *Kring 1812 Års Politik.* Stockholm, 1927. Good; excellent review by A. Schück in *Historisk Tidskrift* (1930), II, 231-251.

Nesselrode, Comte, *Lettres et Papiers.* Paris, 1904-1907.

Oncken, Wilhelm, *Oesterreich und Preussen im Befreiungskriege.* 2 vols., Berlin, 1876.

Pertz, C. H., *Das Leben des Ministers Freiherrn vom Stein.* 6 vols., Berlin, 1851.

Pflugk-Harttung, Julius von, "Bernadotte im Herbstfeldzuge 1813," *Jahrbücher für die Deutsche Armee und Marine, 1905* (vol. CXXVII) Berlin, 1905.

Pingaud, Leonce, *Bernadotte, Napoléon et les Bourbons.* Paris, 1900.

Quistorp, Barthold von, *Geschichte der Nord-Armee im Jahre 1813.* 3 vols., Berlin, 1894.

Raabe, Jens, "Pozzo di Borgo om Karl Johan och Hans Planer 1813," reprinted from *Morgenbladet* in *Lunds Dagblad,* Jan. 2, 1924.

Rein, G., *Adlercreutz,* 2 vols. (publications of Svenska Litteraturessällskapet i Finland, CXCVI), Helsingfors, 1927.

Renier, G. J., *Great Britain and the Establishment of the Netherlands, 1813-1815.* London, 1930.

Sarrans, B. (Jeune), *Histoire de Bernadotte, Charles XIV Jean, Roi de Suède et de Norvège.* 2 vols., Paris, 1845.

Schinkel, Baron von, *Minnen ur Sveriges Nyare Historia.* Ed. by K. V. Bergman and *Bihang* edited by S. J. Boethius. 12 vols., Stockholm, 1854-1855; *Bihang*, 3 vols., Upsala, 1881-1883. This is the "official" history of Carl Johan's regime; interestingly written; contains a large number of documents, all translated into Swedish.

Schück, Henrik (ed.), *Excellensen Grefve A. F. Skjöldebrands Memoarer.* 5 vols., Stockholm, 1904.

Scott, F. D., "Benjamin Constant's Projet Corrigé," *Journal of Modern History*, VII (1935), 41-48.

Scott, F. D., "Bernadotte and the Throne of France, 1814," *Journal of Modern History*, V (1933), 465-478.

Scott, F. D., "Karl Johans Kandidatur till Franska Kronan 1814; några dokument," *Historisk Tidskrift* (1934), häfte III, 271-280.

Sorel, Albert, *L'Europe et la Révolution Francaise.* 8 vols., Paris, 1904.

Sørensen, Carl Th., *Bernadotte i Norden, eller Norges Adskillelse fra Danmark og Forening med Sverig.* 3 vols., Copenhagen, 1903-1904.

Sørensen, Carl Th., *Kampen om Norge i Aaren 1813-1814.* 2 vols., Copenhagen and Christiania, 1871.

Stedingk, (See Björnstierna).

[Suremain] *Mémoires du Lieutenant Général de Suremain (1794-1815).* Paris, 1902.

Tingsten, Lars, *Huvuddragen av Sveriges Krig och Yttre Politik, augusti 1813-januari 1814.* Stockholm, 1924.

Tingsten, Lars, *Huvuddragen av Sveriges Krig och Yttre Politik, januari-augusti, 1814.* Stockholm, 1925.

Tingsten, Lars, *Huvuddragen av Sveriges Yttre Politik, Krigsförberedelser m.m. (1809-1813).* Stockholm, 1923.

Törne, B. O. von, "Frågan om Finland vid Mötet i Åbo, 1812," *Historisk Tidskrift för Finland* (1925), 182-186.

Vandal, Albert, *Napoléon et Alexandre I$^{er}$, L'alliance russe sous le premier Empire.* 3 vols., Paris, 1891-1896.

Varenius, Otto "Kieltraktaten, Dess Genesis," *Historisk Tidskrift* (1931), 129-204.

Villa-Urrutia, Marquès de, *Relaciones entre España é Ingla-*

*terra durante la guerra de la independencia.* 3 vols., Madrid, 1911-1914.

Ward, Sir A. W., and Gooch, G. P., *The Cambridge History of British Foreign Policy 1783-1919.* 3 vols., Cambridge (England), 1922.

Webster, Charles Kingsley, *The Foreign Policy of Castlereagh 1812-1815.* London, 1931.

Woynar, Karl, *Österrikes Förhållande till Sverige och Danmark under åren 1813-1814.* Stockholm, 1892.

# INDEX

# INDEX

# Date Due